AN INCOMPLETE HISTORY OF
ST. JOSEPH COUNTY, INDIANA
AS TOLD THROUGH TWELVE EPIC BIKE RIDES

AARON HELMAN

Cover art:
"St. Joseph River Looking East" by Eugene Kim is licensed under
Creative Commons Attribution 2.0 Generic.

CONTENTS

1. The Center of the New World — 1
2. The First Act of Professor Risley — 21
3. The Nomenclature of the City — 29
4. The Tale of Three Mishawakas — 45
5. The Docked Tail of St. Joseph County — 61
6. A Land of Forgotten Pioneers — 69
7. The Other Side of the River — 83
8. The Wide Shadow of the Golden Dome — 95
9. Titans of Industry — 111
10. Dyngus Day — 129
11. The Vanishing Parts — 141
12. The Whole Thing — 151

To everyone who decided that mine was a life worth saving.

Where the bumble bee sips when the clover is red,
And the zephyrs come ladened with peachblow perfume,
Where the thistledown pauses in search of the rose
And the myrtle and woodbine and wild ivy grows;
Where the catbird pipes up and it sounds most divine
Off there in the branches of some lonely pine:
Oh, give me the spot that I once used to know
By the side of the placid old river St. Joe.

- Ben King (1857-1894)

INTRODUCTION
I NEVER EVEN TOUCHED THE WATER

The river had flowed since long before it ever had a name, long before the first people or the second people found it, long before the third people claimed to be the ones who discovered it. The river hadn't seen history, so much as delivered it, carving a meandering groove into the earth, birthing cities and industry, sculpting a slice of civilization into what we now know as north-central Indiana.

The St. Joseph River flows through the northern part of the county that bears its name; through Osceola, Mishawaka, and South Bend. At a particular spot in South Bend, just north of Cleveland Road; the river flows past the house I grew up in, our front door not more than 200 yards from its muddy shores.

The river flowed past our neighborhood the same way it had flowed past the settlements of the Miami Indian Tribe and later the Potawatomi. These waters would later deliver French and English explorers and fur traders, it would provide attacking routes for invaders and hasten the retreats of the conquered. For a brief time, it would become one of the central hubs of all of the commerce that passed from the Mississippi River and into the northern states and Canada. The river basin also provided the rocks that we hauled up the road in my sister's plastic wagon to landscape around the flowerbeds that dotted our front yard.

For most of my life, the St. Joseph River was just something that was there. I crossed over it several times a day on various bridges to get where I needed to go, but I never felt a pull to explore it, to listen to its stories, to discover the things that it already knew. For the first 35 years of my life, I never even touched the water.

* * *

At some point in my life, after I stopped admiring professional athletes and rock stars above all else, I discovered an affinity for explorers. The idea of *discovering* something awoke a dormant passion inside of me, so I set out to see the world, lamenting only that so much of it had already been discovered and that there was so little left to find.

After living in Indianapolis for six years, I found a friend and we packed our bikes and rolled out on a cross-country trip that lasted 17 days and ended in disaster at a place called Devil's Lake, North Dakota. I landed back in South Bend to start another new life, but I resolved that once I had the time and the means, I would set out to explore the world all over again.

A year became five and then ten and twelve. Along the way I became a husband and a father and then, most recently, a divorcee. During all of it, I found myself admiring different kinds of explorers, personalities like Anthony Bourdain, who could travel the world and explain so perfectly what made each place and each society unique and valuable. I redoubled the promise, telling myself again that once I could explore the world I most certainly would.

I started planning a trip to Vermont. I'd been there once and thought it was neat, so I sketched out the things I would do if I could stay for a month or three. It was a beautiful dream that felt destined to wind up in a notebook of hypothetical adventures, thrown out days after my funeral alongside sets of unblemished journals that I'd always planned to fill in someday. Then I had a thought. It was a thought that rocked my world.

"Why would you think you would explore what you can't when you haven't explored what you could?"

Just like that, the idea was born to explore St. Joseph County, to learn and to share stories, to find adventure. I set out to discover everything I could about the place I lived, the place I was born. There are hundreds of miles of road in the county, just waiting to be ridden. There are towns and histories I'd never discovered even though I had almost always lived here.

Before the rides even began, I poured myself into research that consumed me, and along the way I discovered more about this place than I ever knew existed. I sat in quaint small towns and surveyed prehistoric settlements, I discovered hidden sides of my own city and forgotten stories that needed to see the light of day. I got lost in the inventories of dilapidated cemeteries and learned a history I was never taught in schools. I rode past countless cornfields and chased down midwestern wildlife. I even moved on from the most painful loss of my life.

These twelve bike rides tell a terribly incomplete story of St. Joseph County, but they also tell my story, and I believe that somewhere out there, your story is waiting for you too.

It's probably closer than you think.

*   *   *

For as much time as I spent cycling in St. Joseph County, I've ridden fewer then 25% of its roads. There's so much more left to discover and so much more left to tell. There are libraries full of books that I want to read about the place that I'm from. I hope this book inspires you to discover those stories and to share them yourself. I want to read books about hometown grocers, old theaters, and all of the neighborhoods and great-grandparents that I missed along the way.

If you're looking for somewhere to begin your adventure, feel free to start with mine. Head over to aaronhelman.com/stjoe to download the actual routes for all twelve rides I'll share in this book, and who knows, maybe I'll see you out on the road!

CHAPTER ONE
THE CENTER OF THE NEW WORLD

The river was quiet because the river is always quiet, or at least that's the river I've always known.

Growing up, I never saw boats on the river, but of course I was never looking for them. As it turns out, there is now a public access boat launch just a block from my childhood home. A quick consultation with the DNR reveals that it's actually been there the whole time, and yet somehow my point still stands: I do not ever remember seeing a boat on the water.

Of course, my more recent memories are probably more reliable and they're certainly more plentiful. In the last five years, I've hiked hundreds of miles in St. Pat's Park, many of those with my kids, who have made a ritual of sitting in every single bench at every single overlook along the riverfront. I've had ample opportunity to observe the river, probably in a thousand different instances, usually on the most beautiful days of the entire year.

I've seen dudes on kayaks like twice.

Now I'm here again at St. Patrick's County Park, but I didn't come to hike and I didn't come to stay. I'm here with two of my friends and three of our bikes, standing in a parking lot at the bottom of the sledding hill. My friends are anxious to leave, but I'm not quite ready yet. I'm waiting and I'm watching the river.

There's a boat launch in the lot, evidence that recreational use of the river does take place out there, but none of the kind that I am trying to remember. Legs slung over our top tubes, my companions are eager to set out for the ride. But before we set off to follow a path that once directed the commerce of America's western expansion, I insist on waiting a few moments at the boat launch just to see if the boat traffic ever comes.

It doesn't.

The St. Joseph River is as quiet on this day as I've found it to be on any other day. It flows, but it is not used. It exists, but it is not traversed. The river is quiet. The river is always quiet.

That's what makes it so hard to imagine that this section of the river was once bustling with activity and water traffic, parades of canoes carrying cargo, merchandise, and settlers: an integral part of the most important aquatic highway in the expansion of new world.

We roll out from the park pushing a headwind, not dissimilar from the way the French fur traders would have rowed their canoes upstream from the river's mouth beginning in the 1700s, but they were not the ones who discovered it. The route was known and discovered by Native Americans long before Europeans stepped foot into Indiana, centuries before South Bend was even a place on a map.

Of course, it wasn't called the St. Joseph River at first. It wasn't called the St. Joseph River at second or third either. The white men who stumbled upon it originally called it the River of the Miamis, named after the people who lived along its shores. The Miamis themselves gave the river the name Sakiwäsipi, roughly translated as "the outlet to the lake." The Potawatomi tribe called it Sheggwe, a reference to the legend of an apparition who would appear spontaneously on the riverbank and then vanish just as quickly. Before all of that, in the millennia after the glaciers receded, the river just flowed, never having need for a name at all.

Once it was decided that the river needed a proper European name, at least we can say they gave it an appropriate one. Saint Joseph is the patron saint of, among other things, travelers, explorers, and immigrants. For a very long time, this section of the river would carry many of them.

The first part of our ride skirts the river and hugs its shores, the water only out of sight for a few moments as we ride out of the county park. On a good day, it's not uncommon to spot ospreys and bald eagles soaring overhead, although not in the numbers that Robert de LaSalle and his men would have seen when they passed through this way in December of 1679. Today is not one of those good days. The skies are quiet and empty, although the eagle's nest is visible from the road if you know where to look.

The road is flat and smooth as we roll to a stop and wait for traffic to clear at Auten Road, named for John Auten, the first local casualty in the Civil War. Clear of the stop signs, we pass a few neighborhoods, and then find ourselves gazing upon an ancient-looking series of stonework buildings that used to hang over my elementary school bus rides like a very real haunted house.

The stories they told about Healthwin were sick and maudlin. People had died here, gone crazy here, they said. The sixth graders pointed at the complex across the river and assured me, as a frightened and impressionable first grader, that the place was filled with the ghosts of the deceased.

Now a rehab and long-term care center, the place used to be called Healthwin Hospital; and in the early 1900s, it had a specific purpose. Healthwin was a tuberculosis hospital. Of course they didn't call it that either.

It was a sanatorium.

Maybe the stories were true.

In the medical dark ages, tuberculosis was a disease largely without treatment. Those who suffered were sent away to heal on their own and their exile was less about caring for the sick person and more about keeping the sick person from infecting anyone else.

In 1919, Healthwin hired a new head doctor from Virginia, one who would bring a personal measure of empathy and compassion to the practice. Before he'd ever treated tuberculosis, the doctor had suffered from it. That doctor's name was St. Clair Darden and as we pass the remodeled castle that used to be his hospital, we find ourselves stopped briefly at the road that now bears his name.

Of course, the hospital wasn't here when the Native Americans called this place home. The tuberculosis wasn't here either. That was something that the Europeans would bring, along with guns, capitalism, and Christianity.

We cross the road and roll onto a bike path before we bounce along the wooden floor of the Darden Bridge. According to a historical marker a mile to the east, René-Robert Cavalier, sieur de LaSalle and his men camped beneath what would have been the shadow of this bridge, except that the bridge was not here in 1679.

Actually, the bridge was not even here when it was built in 1885. The old iron truss bridge was originally the passage across LaSalle Street in downtown South Bend. It was 1906 when the single-lane bridge was replaced, deemed insufficient to accommodate the hustle and bustle of the growing city, then floated four miles downstream to its current location, a place then called Mosquito Glen. Mosquito Glen is where I grew up, and although I never heard the moniker as a child, I have to confess, it's not inaccurate.

The floated and re-erected bridge existed as the only river crossing north of the city limits until 1960. In many ways, the Darden Bridge is responsible for the growth and development of Clay and German Townships. Now it stands as a relic of a paved-over past, the last iron truss bridge in St. Joseph County, an unnecessary and romantic crossing that connects handfuls of pedestrians and cyclists from one trail to another.

That second trail skirts the river more closely. Three centuries earlier, we'd have looked here upon a river bustling with activity. Maybe we would have seen a river teeming with splashing fish. Perhaps we would have been startled to see birds of prey, darting like missiles to snatch dinner from the water. The air might have been filled with the whoops of men on boats, Europeans and Native Americans alike, each boat with its own ultimate destination, to places as far north as Newfoundland and as far south as Texas, Louisiana, or the Gulf of Mexico.

But for today, it looks like an empty river, it sounds like a highway, and it smells like shit.

The South Bend Wastewater Facility has been here since 1956 and it's a true miracle of science that the smell of the place doesn't linger more than it does. By all rights, a place that's served 66 years of the city's septic stink should cast a wider and more potent olfactory net than the one we're experiencing today. As it is, we find ourselves rolling into Pinhook Park, the facility still in sight, but its scent a memory already faded.

There's a lake here, but the lake's pretty new. That's because the lake used to be the river. Given the sharp pinhook bend of the St. Joseph River and the cost of construction and upkeep of bridges, engineers decided it would be cheaper, easier, and far more permanent to simply divert the river.

So that's what they did. Steam shovels began dredging a path in 1936, aiming to clear a brand-new riverbed, 750 feet long and 200 feet across. Then, on March 13, 1937, workers detonated 600 pounds of dynamite to finish the job, rattling nearby neighborhoods like a low-grade earthquake as the pent-up river spilled into its new passage.

Typically when man tries to redirect the course of nature, it ends in different degrees of unplanned disaster, but not this time.

By all accounts, the project went off without an obvious long-term impact on the environment and ecosystems surrounding it; certainly not anything worse than the years before 1956 when every sewer drain in South Bend led directly into the river without any treatment of any kind.

Somehow the redirection of the St. Joseph River was entirely successful, accomplishing all of its ambitious civic goals with none of the nasty side effects. Riverside Drive seamlessly connects the northside of South Bend into downtown. The newly created Pinhook Park is a gathering place featuring a fishing lagoon, playgrounds, a walking trail, and a community center. The same birds, fish, and critters live here as did before, urban expansion far more harmful to their numbers than the rerouting of their river.

The only real catch is that, now separate from the place called Pinhook Lagoon, the St. Joseph River no longer contains the one small part of itself that was the most historically significant bit of its 206 miles. In other words, the St. Joseph River no longer touches the place that once lay at the middle of the burgeoning western frontier. It no longer flows quite through what was, once upon a time, the center of the new world.

But it used to.

Our route takes us away from the river, westward along Boland Drive, where we pause briefly to study a stone tablet outside of the Riverview Cemetery. On this day, I notice that someone has left flowers at the base of the stone, believing it to be a tombstone.

It is not a tombstone.

Instead, it's a marker that exists to commemorate the landing spot of Robert Rene Cavalier, Sieur de LaSalle, known as the first white man to set foot in the region.[1] My high school was

---

[1] It seems likely that this is not the case, but we'll get into that a little later.

named after him. The historical record credits him with discovering this spot, a location that would become a critical hub of commerce, politics, and transportation as later generations of pioneers continued their expansion west.

But there's an obvious truth that's been obfuscated by the ones who write the history. Robert de LaSalle was not nearly the first person here. Native Americans from tribes all over the Americas knew this spot. It had been one of the centers of their world for centuries before Columbus commissioned the vessels that would sail to the Americas.

The fact is that LaSalle didn't discover anything here. He didn't stumble upon this place and imprint the first human boot marks along its muddy shores. He came here on purpose, led by a Mohegan Indian guide named White Beaver to traverse the portage the Indians already knew about. The path was travelled so heavily that the ground carved a concave recess between the trees and into the earth, tamped down by centuries of mocassined feet.

Even without the presence of his guide, LaSalle would have noticed the portage as he passed by. He would have noticed the empty space between the trees, the places where Native Americans had cleared brush to make it easier to haul canoes out of the river and up the banks. He would have seen smooth dirt, almost shiny looking, where hundreds or thousands of handmade boats would have been dragged behind a weary paddler bringing home the catch to share with his village.

Despite the heroic narrative that's persisted about the French explorer, LaSalle didn't land here because he had an inkling that it provided the shortest portage to another river that he didn't know existed. He landed here because by sight and by rumor, it would have been obvious that this was the location of something very, very important. By the time he ordered his men to haul their birchbark canoes up from the waters, he would have noticed that every major Indian trail in the area came together at the latitude and longitude where he was standing.

The Potawatomi Trail passed through this spot. So did the Miami Trail. The Ottawa, Illinois, and Chippewas had their own trails through this place. The Great Sauk Trail had a trunk that met right here. Like the extended arms of a great asterisk, every major Native American trail in the area converged here, at the pinhook on the St. Joseph River.

For the sake of his mission, the portage couldn't have come at a better time. LaSalle and his men were running low on provisions. They hadn't eaten meat in days. His crew was turning mutinous and their whispers were becoming too much to ignore. If they hadn't found a buffalo not far from their landing spot, maybe LaSalle's journey would have ended sooner than it did.

LaSalle came here, to the place that is now the Riverview Cemetery, looking to discover an overland route to China. What he found instead was the historical commercial hub of what we now call the Midwest. For their part, the Native Americans who lived there did not realize that they were sitting on a spot that could have been the most lucrative toll booth on the continent. Despite conflicts between Native Americans and Europeans all over the new world, it would appear that peaceful travel through this location was not interrupted until the portage itself was no longer needed.

We pause again, in another cemetery, this time to examine the rotting remains of a tree stump. These are the kinds of things I make my friends do when we ride bikes together. Now rotten from the inside out and filled with rocks to give shape to what remains of the decaying pieces of its trunk, it's hard to believe that this was once a great, enormous tree. It was beneath the shade of this once proud oak that LaSalle signed a treaty with the Great Lakes Indians (including the Potawatomi, Miami, and Illinois tribes). Together, they agreed to resist the encroachment of the aggressive Iroquois Indians, and in exchange for LaSalle's friendship, the tribes agreed to grant LaSalle safe and unfettered passage to explore the Kankakee River. They called it the Council Oak, and now that's the name of a neighborhood, a laundromat, and an antique store. The Council Oak Liquor Store went out of business a long time ago.

By some estimates, the oak tree was over 100 years old when the treaty was signed, which means it would have been more than 400 years old when it was finally felled by a tornado in 1990. Any promise of peace toward the Native Americans that might have been made beneath its branches expired centuries before the tree did.

We roll out of the cemetery to head south on Portage Road. As a baby, it's the first road I ever lived on. My parents live there now. My grandparents are buried on Portage Road. My school bus barreled down Portage Road every single day to take me to every school I ever attended.

I was 37 when I stopped to think about how it got its name.

Once upon a time, before steamboats traversed the Mississippi and before trains crisscrossed the continent, canoes delivered commerce across the new world. Loaded down with men and merchandise and guns and goods, canoes were the easiest and the safest way to cross the continent. After all, it's easier to float things than carry them.

But what happens when one waterway doesn't connect to another? What happens when you need to get from a place serviced by one watershed to a place serviced by another?

There's only one solution. You have to carry your crap to the next river. You have to find a portage, and you have to pray to God that it's not a long portage, because carrying a boat laden with merchandise sucks. It's probably not a problem you've ever thought about, because understanding watersheds isn't a skill that's needed to traverse modern society. I suppose all of that begs the question about why I spent so many miles along Portage Road talking to my friends about watersheds while we cycled through roundabouts and dodged roadkill.

Every waterway north and east of the St. Joseph River belongs to the Great Lakes Watershed. You can explore the rivers in that watershed as much as you want, and plenty of LaSalle's predecessors had, but eventually they'll all dump you back into one of the Great Lakes. They'll never take you any further west or any further south. Of particular importance to Robert de LaSalle, they'll never get you to China.

Fortunately for LaSalle and his men, and for centuries of Native American tribes before him, it was just a four-mile overland hike to connect from the pinhook on the St. Joseph River to the nearest banks of the Kankakee River. For the three of us on our bikes today, it'll be a little farther, but not by much. The Kankakee is a part of the Mississippi River watershed; a watershed that comprises 40% of the landmass of the continental United States and drains parts of 31 states.

European cartologists would later confirm what generations of Native Americans had already known. The four-mile portage was the shortest possible distance to connect the northeast, Great Lakes, and Canada to the Mississippi River; and from there to the south and the west.

If you would have asked me as a middle schooler how Portage Road got its name, I probably would have guessed that there used to be a portage there. I wouldn't have been wrong. But it's even more correct to suggest that Portage Road got its name because it was the site of one of the most crucial portages in the new world, a tightrope strip of land that very literally connected two halves of the continent. Once upon a time, all of it passed through right here. This place was the Crossroads of America long before Indiana was ever a word on a man's lips.

Logistically, in the years before trains and Conestoga wagons, the expansion of a nation was impossible without networked waterways and manageable portages. Those portages were few and far between. They were chokepoints for travelers, gave birth to towns and cities, and became hubs of commerce and industry and culture. This particular portage, no more than a geographical curiosity today, is the catalyst responsible for what would become South Bend. Other portages gave birth to cities like Fort Wayne, Akron, and Chicago; but the overland route we are pedaling through today represented the shortest and most convenient path to connect the continent.

The miles tick along more slowly now as we navigate the bustle of the city. We traverse a network of neighborhoods, once proud, then dilapidated, and now on the verge of revival. We pass by an old church, once my preschool, then closed and sold and opened again, now with a new name and a new theology.

As a child, this was where the fancy grocery store was, the place where the rich kids shopped. When my mom took us there instead of the Kroger, it felt like we'd arrived. Martin's Supermarkets got their start right here in 1947, the flagship store of a grocer that would become an institution throughout the county. But as the money fled the city, Martin's relocated to the suburbs. Their original store sits empty. The corner of Portage and Elwood is a food desert. The road below us is in disrepair and the lots around us are dotted with the shuttered businesses that used to sponsor our Little League teams.

Our ride skirts the near westside of downtown South Bend, past historic churches with rich pasts and tenuous futures. Large stone buildings, constructed as worship spaces for the affluent and well-to-do, now occupy crumbling neighborhoods. Faith leaders are left to bridge the gap between what their congregations once were and what their immediate communities now need them to be.

For a few moments, we find ourselves on an interfaith tour of this stretch of the city, including representations from Protestants, Jews, Muslims, and all matter of Catholics; many of those with their own distinct ethnic histories.

Once we're through to Western Avenue, we pause at a brick building that used to be the Olivet A.M.E. Church, opened in 1873 as the first African American church in South Bend. It would have felt like progress for influential black families like the Powells and Bryants[2] when they founded Olivet as a centerpiece of their burgeoning black community. Finally they had a bit of representation in the mosaic of South Bend's eclectic religious tapestry.

It was the Catholics who got here first. LaSalle was one of them, and as a part of his entourage, he included Father Louis Hennepin, the first priest to set foot in South Bend. A large carving of Hennepin watches over the Riverview Cemetery, even though Hennepin never did anything more than just pass through the place.[3] He never stopped in the area, and it would be more than two centuries before the Catholics planted a parish in South Bend.

---

[2] Just two weeks before this book went to print, John Charles Bryant passed away at the age of 84. Bryant was a direct descendant of the Powell line and a noted historian of South Bend's African American history.

[3] In his extensive writings, Hennepin says little at all about the portage. He is most famous for being known as the first white man to "discover" Niagara Falls.

As for the Native Americans who got here first, their name emblazons the most deeply held religion of my earliest childhood: baseball. Four Winds Field is one of the nicer minor league baseball stadiums in the country, and it provides a tremendous bit of poetry that the team's gift shop is contained in a historically protected Jewish synagogue, the first one in the city. The roof of that synagogue was once the landing spot for a massive home run from Hall of Famer Carlton Fisk; hit when he was on a rehab assignment with the Chicago White Sox.

The team that calls Four Winds Field home is no longer affiliated with the White Sox. Instead it's now home to the South Bend Cubs, the minor league affiliate of the parent team in Chicago, and it's not an inappropriate historical name either. Three centuries earlier, all of this would have been a thick, mature forest. Black bears, which are native to Indiana, would have thrived here. It's virtually certain that bear cubs tromped this ground for centuries before baseball was even a game.

So the earliest pioneers might have contended with bears as they tracked the portage to Kankakee River. For us, it's impatient traffic and a gauntlet of red lights. We dodge potholes and parked cars as we pace down Western Avenue, the air thick with the smell of tacos and exhaust fumes. At times, we bounce along the roads more than we cruise them, but after a few harrowing miles, we pause to stop for a moment at a convenience store held just within the reaching fingertips of the city limits. Here, the bustle of the city fades from view behind us and gives way to a calm grid of farmland up ahead. For a moment, we pause in a parking lot, and I ponder everything that's here right now and lament everything that used to be.

A portage that could shape the discovery of a world requires water on both ends, and as we stop to catch our breaths, I know we're not nearly the first travelers to steal a moment's respite at this precise location. During the centuries before, this spot at the corner of Mayflower and Sample Streets was the put-in at the Kankakee River. Pioneers, merchants, and voyagers would have breathed the same sighs of relief that we do now as we drink from our bottles. The sight of the shores of the Kankakee River meant they didn't have to carry their things anymore. They could float now, and the current would work with them, all the way to the Mississippi River, all the way to Louisiana and the Gulf of Mexico if that's where they wanted to go.

But the put-in isn't here anymore and the Kankakee River isn't even here anymore either. As we gaze at the trappings of the outskirts of the city, it's hard to imagine that this was ever part of one of the most significant swamplands in North America.

Fewer than 200 years ago, this intersection would have belonged to the wetlands. For the fur traders, it would have been heaven: teeming with beaver, deer, bears, mink, turtles, wolves, foxes, otters, and muskrat. Native Americans would have hunted buffalo, lynx, and elk. The birds were so numinous and so thick that their flocks would blot out the sun like an eclipse. During the millennia prior, the marsh was home to mastodons, mammoths, and giant beavers. The thick, muddy waters of the place would protect their remains for modern scientists today.

Once upon a time, the Grand Kankakee Marsh was one of three largest swamps in North America, trailing only the bayou of Louisiana and the Florida Everglades. Its biodiversity was nearly unrivalled.

In the 1800s they called it the Everglades of the North. It was a paradise for hunters and naturalists and for all matter of wildlife. Its lifeblood was the Kankakee River, all 250 miles of it. The Kankakee meandered across western Indiana and into Illinois, and along the way, incomprehensible quantities of life sprung up along its shores.

Lew Wallace, the author of Ben-Hur, described it this way, when he surveyed the Kankakee Marsh for the first time, looking at it from a place not unlike the place I stood with my friends:

> *Never in all my world travels have I seen a more perfect spot nor a more tantalizing river.*

Now it's a 7/11.

It's hard to believe that Presidents and titans of industry sought out this spot ahead of all the others in the world for their hunting expeditions. King Edward VII crossed the Atlantic Ocean just to be here.

But harder to believe still is the historical fact that by the late 1800s, the people who were in charge of things decided that the Grand Kankakee Marsh simply shouldn't exist anymore.

The Swampland Acts of 1849 and 1850 transferred control of localized swamplands from the federal government to the states. That was the beginning of the end. Efforts to dredge the Kankakee River began shortly thereafter. The idea was to straighten the path of the river, to create more space for farmland. Evidently, some asshole[4] looked at a map of Indiana and decided there wasn't enough room in the state to plant corn. Steam shovels and dynamite began to do the same kind of work that would later iron out the

---

[4] While there were many individuals involved in the desecration of the Grand Kankakee Marsh, John Campbell, Indiana's Chief Engineer, was likely more responsible than the rest. It was ultimately under his authority and direction that the dredging of the swamp began. In his view, the Marsh was a mistake to be corrected, and he wrote that the Grand Kankakee Marsh was a "disfigurement" of the land in northwest Indiana.

Pinhook Bend in the St. Joseph River, but on a scale a thousand times bigger.

Typically when man tries to redirect the course of nature, it ends in different degrees of unplanned disaster, but not this time. This disaster was entirely planned. They knew what they were doing and they did it anyway. By the time it was done, the 250-mile Kankakee River had been turned into a 90-mile drainage ditch. 500,000 acres of the best wetlands in North America were wiped out, and the wheels were turning on what may have been the largest part of the largest extinction event in North American history.

In the 1600s, the passenger pigeon was the most prolific bird species throughout North America, maybe throughout the world. It's impossible to conduct a historical census, but ornithologists suggest that a single *flock* of passenger pigeons could number into the billions. It's not hard to imagine LaSalle and his men discharging their weapons while on the hunt and startling a flock of millions of birds into the air. These flocks were enough to darken the sky, a wildlife eclipse that could have lasted for hours. The historical record even takes care to note the impressive amount of dung created by these flocks, comparing it to something like a snowfall.

The Grand Kankakee Marsh was among the favorite breeding grounds for the passenger pigeon, and it's not difficult to draw a straight line from the dredging of the marsh to the death of Martha, the last surviving passenger pigeon. She succumbed to a stroke while in captivity at the Cincinnati Zoo in 1914. The scope of the extinction is equally impressive and terrifying. It took fifty years to turn some five billion birds into zero.

But it's not just the passenger pigeon that was lost. The Grand Kankakee Marsh was once home to the largest Black Oak Savannah in the world. Elk used to roam the marshlands and much of northern Indiana. Countless mammal, bird, fish, tree, and flower species were wiped out in the effort. It is not wrong, nor is it hyperbole to suggest that the dredging of the Grand Kankakee Marsh was an ecological genocide.

I need you to know, as I write this paragraph, that I am angry and I am sad and I am a little drunk. The bike ride through the cornfields was fine, but those cornfields never should have been there. This was supposed to be the most important and most enduring wetland in the northern half of the United States, but they murdered it. They murdered it and it's not coming back.

*   *   *

Crumstown persists as one of the many broken promises of the dredging of the Kankakee River. Once a heralded entry point to some of the richest hunting grounds in the entire marsh, Crumstown was a destination for sportsmen as far afield as New York, Washington D.C., and Europe. But the civil engineers who came with the steam dredgers promised something more. A 1907 History of St. Joseph County predicted that Crumstown would "grow to a place of considerable importance."

It did not.

At least it used to be more than it is now. Crumstown was platted by Christian Holler in 1875 and was originally named Crum's Point in honor of his wife's family. Holler would later become a state senator. The town he founded would later change its name to Crumstown, an effort to halt the post office confusion that consistently sent its mail to Crown Point, Indiana instead. At its peak, Crumstown was located on a new-fangled gravel road and had its own hotel, post office, and baseball team. A crude velodrome hosted cycling races featuring professional riders.

Today, Crumstown is largely a ghost town. Both of its grocery stores burned down in the 1930s and neither were replaced. Both of its schools sit empty, the velodrome and baseball park are flattened. The gas station is shuttered.

The place has a bar and grill; now for sale and in need of an owner. One church is closed and another is still open. Crumstown's current population not more than the 100 who lived here in 1900. The land is flat and farmed and does not whisper of the marshland that used to cover this part of the earth. It forgets the Indian village that thrived just a bit further up the road.

The only hint of Crumstown's rich ecological past is found a mile further south, adjacent to a cemetery that holds more gravestones than Crumstown holds people. The County Parks Department maintains a boat launch here, and if my friends and I had portaged our canoes as far as this, we'd be able to put out into the Kankakee River now, more than six miles away from the original spot.

I had expected to be underwhelmed by the sight of the river once we found it again. I'd read and read about the mighty Kankakee and the marvel that was the Grand Kankakee Marsh. I'd also read about its demise. I didn't come to the Jasinksi Boat Launch expecting much. I knew it would be bad.

Somehow, it was so much worse than that. To call this a boat launch is a generous use of those words. In fact, the boat launch is not more than a very small hill that someone cleared with a weed whacker. I guess that's all the boat launch you need when you're trying to put out into an overgrown drainage ditch.

As I looked around, peered at the water under the bridge and studied the farmland that had collapsed in all around me, I tried to imagine what this place would have looked like 150 years prior, teeming with life and vegetation.

My imagination failed me. Corn grew here in neat rows as if it always had and as if it always would, as if that was the land was made for. We were surrounded by a swath of earth with no greater purpose than to provide feed for cattle. What was once here will never be seen again.

Or maybe not.

A strange thing happens as we turn onto New Road. The land on either side of the road feels different. It feels wilder. The road beneath our bikes is undoubtedly less maintained. The humidity rises enough to be noticed. And everywhere around us, there are signs that the swamp is trying to return.

The Pokagon Band of Potawatomi Indians have a story all their own. Saved from forced deportation by the decision of Chief Leopold Pokagon to convert his band to Roman Catholicism; the Pokagon Band was able to remain in the land of their ancestors in lower Michigan and northwest Indiana. Now recognized as a sovereign Indian Nation with more than 4000 citizens; the modern Pokagon band continues to have an impact on the culture and economy of St. Joseph County.

They're also having an impact on the land. In 2003, the Pokagon Band enrolled more than 1,100 acres of the former marsh into the federal Wetland Reserve Program. A decade later, efforts were begun to restore the land. Strategic scrapes of the land are creating environments ripe for wetland plants and animals. Given enough time, the marshland will begin to return. In fact, as we cycle down the pockmarked road, there's evidence that it's already happening.

Wetland foliage is thriving in the protected area. It's a stark and visible contrast to the previous miles, even to the untrained eye. The wildlife census shows massive changes as animals like ospreys, once plentiful here, are beginning to return. It's a hopeful place for those who celebrate biodiversity.

And yet, as the protected land finds its border at the western edge of St. Joseph County and the burgeoning marsh gives way to another set of neatly lined farms, it feels like a very noble, but very small effort. Indeed, the Pokagon Band was given just 0.2% of a marsh that used to span a half-a-million acres. The passenger pigeons will never return; and it will take a much larger intervention if these lands will ever see grazing buffalo again.

As we pause on the bridge that marks the end of St. Joseph County, we look over the Kankakee River one more time. It's not mighty, but it's more of a river than the ditch we found back at the boat launch. This is the place where generations of travelers, explorers, hunters, and traders would have left the boundaries of the place that would become St. Joseph County; and as the rain begins to fall on us, almost as if on cue, it's the place we'll turn around to head back for home.

CHAPTER TWO
THE FIRST ACT OF PROFESSOR RISLEY

We pull our bikes from the Jeep atop a gravel parking lot that exists to showcase a place that has existed for thousands of years, and somehow, has only just been found. I am fascinated with this place, fascinated with the idea that something can still be *discovered*, in a long-settled part of the country. And the fact that all of it is within eyeshot of a numbered highway? That's still difficult for me to comprehend.

It's a bit of a hyperbole to say that the Lydick Bog lay undiscovered until 2016. In fact, Father Julius Nieuwland, a chemistry professor at Notre Dame, wrote of its existence all the way back in 1913. It just wasn't regarded among his more important accomplishments, so the memory of his writings slipped away into the forgotten parts of the university library.

Probably that's not surprising. Nieuwland is more famous in chemistry circles for his work in synthetic rubber and for discovering the processes that would lead to the invention of neoprene. Around St. Joseph County, he's probably more notable for being professor and mentor to a certain, young Notre Dame student named Knute Rockne.[5]

Given all that, maybe it's not so surprising that Nieuwland's hobby work in botany went unnoticed and largely forgotten for over 100 years. It was 2014 before local botanists began expressing their

---

[5] Equally mind-boggling is that the two would later become teaching colleagues. Knute Rockne graduated Notre Dame with a pharmacy degree, then returned as a professor in chemistry while becoming the most storied coach in the history of the university's football team.

interest in finding the bog, and in 2016; the land was purchased by the Shirley Heinze land trust. Shortly thereafter, the bog was rediscovered, catalogued by botanists, and listed as a protected area by its new purchasers.

A bog is a different kind of environment compared to swamps and other wetlands. Even during the heyday of the Grand Kankakee Marsh, the Lydick Bog was distinct and separate. Here the soil is more acidic and less oxygenated, leading to a distinct evolution pattern for the plants that call the bog home. In order to survive, they had to learn to eat insects. The Lydick Bog is the only such environment within the limits of St. Joseph County and it's the only place to find carnivorous plants.

As fascinated as I am with the story of the bog, it's just a few moments before we're rolling away from the thing and onto the shoulder of US 20, the first road in America that connected the Atlantic to the Pacific. We won't follow the road for long, and in fact we're turned off of the busy highway within a mile as we roll south along Quince Road.

A few miles south of the bog, we find ourselves in Lydick proper. It's a small community and functions largely as a kind of rural outpost within the greater South Bend Area. If Lydick has a downtown, you'll find it at the corner of Edison and Quince; home to the Methodist church, a pair of restaurants, and not far from the fire station. The tones of the church bells ring out as we pass through, but we are the only ones who attend the parade.

A pair of lakes – the North and South Chain Lakes – provided the building blocks of the pioneer community that started here in the 1830s, but human civilization has roots that run deep. These lakes were once home to a people even more ancient than the Native Americans. Long before this place was ever called Lydick, the Mound Builders simply called it home.

Known for their distinct practice of burying their dead in massive earthwork piles, these sites were sought out by historians, collectors, and treasure hunters alike. Massive numbers of bronze axes came from the mound discovered on South Chain Lake, and as they are wont to do, later settlers would continue to pick the site clean. The last known artifacts were plucked from the Lydick mound sometime in the 1970s, and I struggled to find wherever the mound used to be or any locals who remembered how to find it. So much of history seems so unimportant until it's gone.

Probably the most fascinating bit of Lydick's history is the controversy surrounding its name, or better put, the controversy surrounding its names. First the community was called Warren Center, named after the railroad station within its limits. Next, they called it Sweet Home as that was the name of the Post Office. The two names existed concurrently through the second half of the 1800s, and if that wasn't confusing enough, by the turn of the century, it would gain another pair of names.

In 1901, a blacksmith named Irvin Lydick ordered a sleigh to be shipped from Sears and Roebuck.[6] Unfortunately, due to confusion with the railroad, his package was sent instead to the town of Warren, Indiana. The sleigh wouldn't arrive at Warren Center until spring, after the snow had melted. An incensed Lydick launched a complaint with the railroad. In order to make things right with the jilted blacksmith, the railroad renamed the station in his honor; further evidence that customer service isn't what it used to be.

After the renaming of the station, some in the community began to follow suit. For them, Lydick became the name of their town. However, it wasn't a consensus opinion. Mina Lindley, whose

---

[6] A blacksmith ordering a sleigh from Sears & Roebuck might be the most 1901 thing that has ever happened anywhere in America.

husband Ashbury Lindley ran the Sweet Home Post Office, was furious, and demanded that the town be named in honor of her husband and their family. After carrying a pair of competing names for the first seventy years of its history, now they were carrying a second and distinct pair of competing names.

The debate was intense, but brief. By 1913, the Post Office was closed, although frustrations with the burgeoning community's identity crisis probably had nothing to do with it. The name Lydick has appeared to stick, and before I can finish sharing the full story of the area's historical nomenclature with my friends, we have already passed through the place and are exploring a new part of the map. The echoes of the church bells are faded away by the time we point our bikes west and roll into another grid of neatly stacked farms. At Larrison Boulevard, we find ourselves trapped behind a loaded combine, holding our breaths and keeping our distance to avoid eating the chaff thrown off by the wind.

Like much of the county, this is an agricultural area, interrupted only occasionally by the remnants of settlements that never quite achieved the status they once expected. Places like Olive and Ziegler popped up at the intersections of railroads and busier agricultural cross-streets.

Once the railroads consolidated their routes and reduced their stops, these micro-communities found themselves bereft of an identity, reduced to little more than a four-way stop and a bumpy railroad crossing. But it could have been worse. When the Northern Indiana Railway made the decision to bypass a place called Hamilton altogether, the community disintegrated into forgotten obscurity. You'll find it on a map, but when you roll through, there is just nothing there.

The cornfields don't quite last forever, and soon enough, farmlands turn into homes and homes turn into neighborhoods. A

Serbian Orthodox Monastery is the last quiet vestige of the country before a right turn on Timothy Road delivers us into the relative bustle of the town of New Carlisle. One small hill and then another places us within the town's narrow limits and provides the opportunity to remember one of the more bizarre stories of one of St. Joseph County's founding fathers.

In 1835, at the ripe age of 21 years, Richard Risley Carlisle, a born-and-bred New Englander, paid $2,000 to buy the 160 acres of land that would become the town that bore his name – New Carlisle. He platted the town and named its streets after streets from his beloved Philadelphia. He married and built a small a cabin near Filbert and Front Streets, then proceeded to begin the important work of creating the skeleton of the town that still stands today.

Then he ran away to join the circus.

It's not entirely known why Carlisle made such an abrupt about-face. The man himself was illiterate and so there is no record of his own correspondences because he had none. A St. Joseph County historian dug deep to discover a few nuggets that might help explain why Carlisle up and left. It's known he had a failed run for the state legislature, faced a lawsuit from his brother-in-law, and later declared bankruptcy. Carlisle lost two young children, both of whom were buried in the churchyard behind the First Methodist Church. The iron cross that marked their burial spot was rediscovered in the church's basement more than 150 years later.

Carlisle's time in his town appears to have largely been marked by tragedy and personal misfortune, reason enough for the man to desire a fresh start.

So by 1841, Carlisle was touring the county as an acrobat and juggler, working under the name Professor Risley. He is touted by the Guinness Book of World Records as the inventor of the Risley Act, in which he would lie on his back and juggle children with his feet. The act was a hit, and Professor Risley would go on to perform for Queen Victoria and Prince Albert. He was also internationally known as a skilled marksman and put together his own travelling show in England, wowing crowds with his abilities to blow away targets.

Remarkably, founding a town and naming it after himself would not nearly be the most notable thing that Richard Risley Carlisle did in his life. He would go on to work in Australia and New Zealand as a gold panner. He lived mysteriously in Singapore for a few years, then reemerged as a circus performer in Shanghai.

Then he did something that would really change the world in ways that reverberate throughout American culture today.

In 1864, at the age of 50, Richard Risley Carlisle took his act to Japan, becoming the first professional Western acrobat in the country. His act was popular and it drove circus culture to sweep through Japan, but his impact went beyond the travelling show. It's almost a footnote to his life, but Carlisle is individually credited with introducing ice cream to Japan.

Carlisle connected with traditional Japanese acrobats and performers, then went on to create his "Imperial Japanese Troupe" of acrobats and jugglers. Three years after he set foot in Japan, Carlisle was embarking with his new crew on a World Tour. They would go on to perform across the United States and Europe, counting Presidents and kings and queens among their patrons. Legend has it that Carlisle passed through New Carlisle just once more in his life, a whistle stop while touring with the Imperial Japanese Troupe. If the story is to be believed, he looked around and promised to return again someday.

He never did.

The impact of Professor Risley's "Imperial Japanese Troupe" is almost impossible to overstate. Author Frederik Schodt draws a straight line from Carlisle's tour to America's persistent fascination with Japanese culture and our current obsession with everything from anime to manga to Pokémon. Not bad for a man who didn't even know how to read.

As fascinating as all of that is, the town of New Carlisle does not carry much of the frivolity of Carlisle's second act as a circus magnate. Instead it is filled with the kind of German sensibility that concerns itself with practical things and yeasty beers. The town is fighting to maintain its identity, and many within it are pushing hard against the development of something called the Indiana Economic Corridor.

Yard signs decry the creation of the IEC and the industrial parks it promises to bring with it. The people who call New Carlisle home live here because they enjoy the pace of a small-town kind-of-life. They aren't like Richard Risley Carlisle. The eponymous founder of their town was an opportunist, a serial entrepreneur, and a capitalist through and through. He would likely be a proponent of the IEC, but his vote doesn't count anymore. After all, Carlisle left. He left and he never came back.

When Richard Risley Carlisle died, his will indicated that he should be buried in the place he most considered home; and that wasn't in the town that bore his name. Instead, Carlisle was buried at the Mount Moriah Cemetery in Philadelphia. The histories of his life only mention New Carlisle as a passing curiosity.

As we roll north of town along County Line Road, we find ourselves straddling a pair of time zones and waiting on a pair of trains. Further beyond the town's limits, just shy of the state line, we swing into the Spicer Lake Nature Preserve, one of the purest reminders of what this area used to be and what economic development threatens to take away all over again.

The preserve is home to a pair of lakes, and I'd argue, the best frog-spotting in all of St. Joseph County. A boardwalk skirts Spicer Lake and manicured trails pass through an old-growth forest. The county parks own this place and it's not going to be taken away, but none of the preserve exists very far from the road. Economic development, left unchecked, could threaten the same peace and quiet here that the residents of New Carlisle hold onto so tenuously.

Progress is inevitable, and if not the IEC, it will be something else later on. New Carlisle is situated on a straight line that bridges the gap between South Bend, Gary, and Chicago. It's too strategic a location to stave off growth forever. Economic development is coming; organically, if not nudged along by the hand of a meddling county government. The challenge for New Carlisle will be hanging on to its small-town identity while inevitably becoming a more important industrial hub. Maybe in all of this, they can take a lesson from their founder.

They're going to have to learn how to juggle two things at the same time.

CHAPTER THREE
THE NOMENCLATURE OF THE CITY

The founding of the community that would become South Bend, Indiana was neither an accident nor a coincidence. It was inevitable. It was always inevitable. The only miracle is that it took so long. It's a story that begins at a familiar place, and once again we find ourselves outside of the Riverview Cemetery, surveying the place where LaSalle and his men first landed their boats, the northern gate of the historic nation-building portage.

Of course, there's nothing left of LaSalle's journey. The portage is gone and grown over. The Kankakee River is gone. Robert de LaSalle is long gone, killed in a mutiny eighteen years after he first stepped foot in what is now Indiana, his clothes stripped from him, his body left for the vultures somewhere in Texas.

But as we pilot our bikes south down Portage Road, once again retracing the route of the French explorer, the echoes of LaSalle's influence are everywhere. LaSalle Street is one of the major thoroughfares through the city. Apartments and beers and fancy restaurants are named in his honor. The repurposed historic Hotel LaSalle sits at the west end of the LaSalle Street Bridge.

We're going to see all of those things during the course of this ride, but before we can do that, I've decided that we need to go somewhere else, to see another piece of history, this one more personal.

For the first time in 20 years, I'm going back to high school.

LaSalle High School used to be known as the pride of the westside, but it's fair to say that its glory days were long gone by the time I arrived. It wasn't that our crop didn't have cream. It did. The years surrounding mine produced star athletes, a Daytona 500 winner, and even an Olympic gold medalist. But fewer than half of us were graduating, and by the time I was rolling toward my own commencement, the decision had been made to close the school altogether.[7]

Now we're rolling north on Elmer Street past tightly bunched houses and narrow roads lined with unmoving cars. Abandoned and unkempt homes dot the neighborhood. Boarded windows send a message that this is a part of town in need of a lift, but recent legislature has prioritized development and revitalization in other parts of the city. Like so many other things, it didn't used to be this way.

During the years of legal and formal racism; banks, property sellers, and even realtors stood against the integration of neighborhoods. African Americans were consigned to slums. But in the 1950s, beginning with a series of secret meetings among Studebaker employees, there was a movement to make all of that change.

This group of brave African Americans realized they only had power as a collective. A bank couldn't risk backlash over a single mortgage, but it would be impossible to turn down the profits of a large conglomerate. The black families who hosted the secret meetings pooled their money together. They formed a non-profit called Better Homes South Bend and targeted a block for development right here on Elmer Street. Money gave them power, and they marched into boardrooms and dared the banks to turn them down.

---

[7] During my senior year of school, an arson incident torched half of the building. It was a busy year.

The banks accepted the dare, at least for a while. The FHA sent in a ringer to help mount public pressure against their discriminatory practices. That, combined with the promise of profit, led the banks to cave. The homeowners lined up construction of the Better Homes Neighborhood in South Bend. We're riding through the place now, but it still feels like there's a long way to go. This road and these houses were once imagined as the centerpiece of racial progress. If that's ever what it was, it doesn't feel that way anymore.

The LaSalle Area, as the neighborhood is now known, is in need of a lifeline, and even the roads beneath our rolling wheels are screaming out for care. They send shockwaves through our spines as we jostle and jump over cracks and potholes. The city has chosen different priorities in different places; and it's hard not to wonder if the men and women who fought for their Better Homes would recognize their neighborhood today or if they'd even see the progress they worked so hard to make.

Even Robert de LaSalle, the man these blocks are named after, has lost some of the luster from his name. Historians have begun to revisit the idea that he was the first white man to visit this place. Some books and some historians have declared with certainty that he was not. In discussions that are not without controversy, some have even suggested that historical markers be rewritten to reflect that uncertainty.

But if Robert de LaSalle wasn't the first European to discover this place, then who was? Almost certainly it was a Frenchman, and the most likely other candidate is Jacques Marquette. He never wrote specifically about the area, but his companions did include the St. Joseph River on a crude map that predates LaSalle by more than five years. Marquette was making a return trip into Michigan from the Mississippi River, most likely through the Kankakee and then the St. Joseph. If he managed to bridge those two watersheds without utilizing the ancient portage, it means he took a pretty terrible route to do so. The most likely truth is that Marquette got here first, traversed the portage with the help of his Indian guide, and wandered the path that passes the school that now bears his name.

The old Marquette School is nearing its hundredth birthday against all odds. The school system wanted to tear it down. So did the mayor. But it's still there, historically protected by a set of loopholes that removed the mayor's veto power. There are no plans to restore the building, and like much of the area, it's empty, abandoned, and boarded up. A new Marquette Montessori Academy stands at the other end of the property, and like so much of the history before it, the original building stands silenty in its place, waiting to fall down.

Our route points us back toward the Riverview Cemetery, the site of the portage, the place that would inevitably birth a great city. Given the strategic location of the portage, the intersection of a half-dozen Native American hunting trails, and the capitalistic pragmatism of European pioneers, it was only a matter of time before settlers would smell opportunity and choose to build a home here.

There was money to be made at the southern bend of the St. Joseph River and there were three men who would become among the first to make it. Pierre Navarre, Alexis Coquillard, and Lathrop Taylor came out here to make their money trading furs; and each of them would be buried here and become known as one of the founding fathers of South Bend.

No longer stymied by grids of degraded roads and a parade of four-way stops, we're able to get up to speed as we pedal along Lathrop Street, named after the least famous of the trio of pioneers who helped build South Bend into what it is today. It's a minor road and does little more than connect Portage to Bendix. Curiously, the road carries Taylor's first name instead of his last.

Lathrop Taylor was an agent working in the fur trade for Samuel Hanna & Co.; and while the decision to build an outpost here in 1827 was no more prescient than the decision to build a Starbucks or a gas station at a busy intersection, perhaps Taylor had more foresight than he is given credit for. His choice to erect a trading post on the land that now holds South Bend's Century Center meant he was doing business three miles upstream from the historic portage. But as roads and trails were built and perfected, aquatic travel became less and less important. By the 1830s, Michigan Street meant that South Bend was open for business, and the trails that ran between Fort Wayne and South Bend would soon come to carry more commerce than the river.

Or maybe it wasn't the foresight of Lathrop Taylor that landed him in the place that would become the center of downtown South Bend. That's because, in the true spirit of American capitalism, he was only copying the person who got here first – Alexis Coquillard.

Coquillard Elementary School sits west of downtown South Bend, beyond Bendix Road and near the airport. It's a harrowing ride down a concrete pad of a road, but we enjoy a few moments as we gaze across a clear view of planes landing on the runway. My dad used to work out here, and so did I a few times, loading and unloading pallets of frozen foods from semi-trucks before they found their homes in a deep fryer at a TGI Friday's. The warehouse has been bought and sold, acquired and reacquired. I don't know what happens in that building now. I don't even care enough to Google it.

Our tour of the airport district finds its climax at my first elementary school. I spent the first four years of my educational career as a Coquillard Comet,[8] and I remember learning about Alexis Coquillard during units on local history with Mrs. Jackman.

Coquillard was as American as anyone could be in the 1820s, and as a sixth-generation American, his family line was far older than the nation itself. As an agent of John Jacob Astor's American Fur Company, Coquillard set up shop in South Bend in 1823, a full four years before Lathrop Taylor. Overland routes were not yet in vogue and the river was still king for those moving goods across the continent. Coquillard (or his bosses) recognized that there was opportunity near the portage, and it's not hard to imagine why. Astor and Coquillard would have realized they could make profit by exploiting the most enduring truth of human nature; that people were lazy.

The weight of a trapper's wares is of little concern when he is floating down a river. But confronted with a portage and the prospect of hauling everything in a wagon for four miles? That created motivated sellers. Early traders in South Bend played the same game as early traders at every major portage. Faced with carrying their crap, travelers became desperate to unload their goods. If trappers bound for Texas or New Orleans arrived in South Bend with more cargo than they could carry, they had little choice but to sell their excess inventory for whatever price Coquillard would offer. Similarly, northbound merchants who'd had bad luck along the Mississippi were forced to buy goods from Coquillard at his price or else return to Canada empty-handed.

That part wasn't in my first-grade picture book.

---

[8] By fourth grade, I was a John F. Kennedy Roadrunner. Kennedy was an assassinated U.S. President who had no particular tie to Indiana. The roadrunner is a bird that lives in the desert. I have no idea who is in charge of making these kinds of decisions.

Taylor and Coquillard were adversaries in business, employed by rival companies, and yet they would become the two fathers of South Bend. Coquillard was the more successful trader. Taylor was the more successful businessman, operating a profitable general store and tavern in addition to his trading ventures. Coquillard's entrepreneurship was more of a mixed bag. He failed spectacularly at an attempt to reroute the Kankakee into the St. Joseph, leaving banks little choice but to foreclose on him. His attempt to build a boat to deliver flour from his mill in South Bend all the way to Lake Michigan was a similar disaster. The boat was too heavy to float along the river.

But no matter his failures, there would be money in furs, as long as the fur trade was still alive. Alexis Coquillard was held in high esteem among the Indian tribes, and they were always willing to pass their best deals to him instead of Taylor. A legend tells that a local band of Indians offered to make Coquillard their chief but that Coquillard declined the offer. Years later, Coquillard would leverage those friendships while fighting his own moral battle. The government had placed Alexis Coquillard in charge of removing all of the Native Americans from St. Joseph County.

In 1831, Coquillard and Taylor put aside their disparate business interests to formally plat and found a town; forming a police department, and appointing Ben Potter and Thomas Skiles as constables. It wasn't a moment too soon. Competing towns were being platted nearer the historic portage, first the town of St. Joseph and later the town of Portage. Both of these could have absorbed South Bend instead of the other way around, but Coquillard and Taylor both lobbied to have their town made the county seat. Their appeal was successful, and soon enough South Bend was swallowing up the places that had tried to challenge it.

That doesn't mean the first years of the city were without controversy. The name South Bend wasn't popular with everyone, and when the first Post Office referred to the town as "Southold," there was a movement to adopt Southold as the town's official moniker. It was a simpler time, when the greatest civic difficulty was arguing about whether or not the name of your town was stupid. The population of Southold in its first official year was 128. The next year, the place officially declared that it would be called South Bend.

It's just a few moments away from Coquillard School when the downtown skyline comes into view. It's hard to imagine a time when this place was home to ten dozen people. And then, as we navigate Vassar Avenue and point ourselves toward the historic Leeper Park, it's harder still to imagine the places that those people called home.

The first permanent European resident of St. Joseph County was Pierre Navarre. He preceded Coquillard in his work for the American Fur Company and after several successful trading trips through the area in the 1810's, he decided it was worth turning the place into his home. He established a trading post, erected a log cabin, married a Potawatomi woman, and fathered six children. The log cabin, the first of its kind within the county limits, is still standing, preserved on the east side of Leeper Park. Less than the length of a long jump and half as wide, Navarre's cabin is a reminder of a different way of life. Once upon a time, it would have taken twenty of these things to house the full population of South Bend.

Navarre may have been the first white man here, but unlike Coquillard and Taylor, he wasn't so interested in forming a town. In fact, as he aged, he found himself identifying less with the European-descended Americans and more with the Potawatomi people he married into. When tribes were forcibly relocated in the 1840s, Navarre went with them, saying, "I am only an Indian."

The development of South Bend happened at an alarming pace. It was 1820 when the white people moved in and 1838 by the time the Potawatomi tribe was rounded up, marched out, and relocated to a reservation in Kansas, along a path that would become known as the Trail of Death. The ugly and shameful incident is likely the darkest moment in the history of the county.

South Bend had transformed from a trading post into a burgeoning metropolis in barely a decade. By the end of the 1840s, it was about to make a national impact, the first domino in a chain of many that might have led to the beginning of the Civil War. We navigate again through the city, to a courthouse not too far away. There's a historical marker here that remembers J. Chester and Elizabeth Allen, a husband-and-wife team of African American lawyers who worked with Better Homes South Bend and did much of the hard work to help integrate their hometown during the middle part of the 1900s. But it's actually a different racial injustice we're here to remember now, one that would make South Bend a part of the conversation in the affairs of the nation.

In 1849, a Kentucky slave owner named John Norris brought to conclusion a mission to reclaim six slaves who had escaped two years prior. He'd managed to locate Lucy and David Powell[9] along with four of their children, in Cass County, Michigan; just a few miles north of South Bend.

Under cover of night, Norris and eight of his men burst into the Powell cabin with their guns drawn, shackled the people he called his property, and began the long march back across Indiana.

---

[9] Lucy and David Powell are not related to the Powell family who were influential in founding Olivet AME Church, the first African American church in South Bend.

The people of South Bend made sure he wouldn't make it very far. A sympathetic lawyer procured a hasty writ from a judge, ordering Norris to release the Powells. Norris and his men were armed to the teeth and were inclined to fight their way out of trouble, but a ruckus had formed all around. In moments, Norris and his men were surrounded on all sides by a gaggle of South Benders. They were not on his side. Norris relented, hired a lawyer, and fought in the courts. It was a tense and ugly trial, and it did not end the way that John Norris wanted it to. The judge declared that Norris had not sufficiently proven his ownership of the Powell family and ordered them to be freed.

Then all hell broke loose.

Norris brandished a gun, because in the 1840s, you could bring a gun into court with you. He shouted that he was taking the Powells with him and that he would shoot anyone who stood in his way. Amazingly, it wasn't an uninformed or impetuous decision. Norris was acting on legal counsel. In fact, his lawyer was standing on a table, berating the citizens of South Bend, and advising his client to "shoot all who interfere".

Unfortunately for Norris, there was a lot of interference. Nearly 200 people had assembled to stand between Norris and the Powells, and Norris didn't have that many bullets. Once again, he was forced to back down. This time the Powells were free for good.

But the story doesn't quite end there. Norris would go on to file suits with higher courts for lost property. He won those suits and recovered thousands of dollars from the individuals who had interfered, including local abolitionists like Almond Bugbee and Solomon Palmer; amounts that would have been ruinous for them.

The trial would gain national prominence for exposing loopholes in the 1793 Fugitive Act and would lead to passage of a harsher Fugitive Act in 1850. That act led directly to the publication of <u>Uncle Tom's Cabin</u>, which, according to Abraham Lincoln, led to the Civil War.

But in the years between the South Bend Slave Trials and the beginning of the Civil War, South Bend was unaware of and unfocused on its place as a kind of lynchpin in American affairs. It was only concerned with growth, and it was growing quickly.

The pace of progress makes itself apparent in so many different and unexpected ways. For example, the historic throttling brick roads that line the Chapin Park National Historic District remind you in violent and visceral ways that road surfacing technology has evolved quite a bit since the middle part of the 1800s. I realize quickly that my narrow bike tires aren't built to navigate roadways like this one and that my spine isn't built to bear them.

But nowhere is the pace of development more apparent than the very short ride between Navarre's log cabin at Leeper Park and the Horatio Chapin House on Park Street. The 4,000 square foot home is the crown jewel of the historic neighborhood that bears his name. The eaves of its roof soar above a row of well-manicured trees. The home is striking, even today, and it's unsurprising that the place sold in 2018 for more than half-a-million dollars.

Chapin's influence in South Bend went far beyond his stately home. He operated the first general store in the area, founded the first church, and was the first president of South Bend's trustees. He was also the first president of the St. Joseph County Historical Society, and without his early efforts to catalog and preserve history, much of the book you're reading right now would not have been written.

As a boon for his successes, Chapin began construction on his distinctive home in 1855 and the job was completed by 1857.

There were fewer than forty years between Navarre's sparse cabin and Chapin's gorgeous mansion. South Bend was not just growing. It was exploding.

One has to imagine what it must have been like for an aging Pierre Navarre. After the death of his wife on the reservation, Navarre returned to a South Bend that looked nothing like the one he remembered. From the place his cabin originally stood, he might have seen the Chapin House soaring high above the trees on the other side of the river. So much had changed in so little time

We jostle our way through Chapin Park, navigate around the back end of the downtown medical district, and turn right onto Charles Martin Drive, named after a more recent hero. Martin was a fierce advocate for urban youth and his road takes us toward another historic district with another historic name.

Schuyler Colfax was a politician of national prominence, first a Whig and then a Republican in the United States House of Representatives. But before all of that, he was a newspaperman in South Bend, Indiana. Even before that, he was a teenager, working at the New Carlisle Post Office in the years before Richard Risley Carlisle ran away to join the circus. It's a virtual certainty that the two knew each other and a remarkability that of New Carlisle's first fifty residents, one would become an international superstar and another would help guide America through and beyond the Civil War. When Professor Risley's Imperial Japanese Troupe returned in the 1860s to tour the United States, Carlisle might have seen the old post office boy in a suite of honor during one of his shows. After all, Schuyler Colfax had become the Vice President of the United States.

Schuyler Colfax came to political power during the most fraught time in American history. Elected to the House in 1855 while Horatio Chapin was building a house all of his own; Colfax would go on to become Speaker during the presidency – and assassination – of Abraham Lincoln. He was Vice President during Ulysses Grant's term. And if not for an abrupt about-face, he might have become the President of the United States during the last years of America's Reconstruction Era.

In the 1800s, candidates ran for the Vice Presidency in the same way as, and separately from, the President. Since Colfax had aspirations for the higher office, he stated in 1870 that he would not be running for a second term as Vice President. Grant had mentioned privately that he would likely not seek a second term and Colfax sought to be the one who would replace him.

But Grant would ultimately choose to run again. He would win easily. By the time Colfax tried to sneak back into the race for Vice President, it was too late. He lost his campaign, not without controversy, and would never run for office again. Colfax would return to South Bend, and though he would crisscross the country as a traveling lecturer, South Bend would remain his home for the rest of his life.

Colfax appears to be worthy of the honor his home city has bestowed upon him. His politics were palatable and, for his time, even honorable. He was fervently anti-slavery and held radically progressive views about Reconstruction. Colfax's name marks a prominent street and a now-closed school. As we pull into the South Bend City Cemetery, we're confronted with his gravesite near the entrance and a modest stone that also bears his name.

We leave the cemetery and find ourselves once again on LaSalle Avenue before we turn north toward the Near Northwest neighborhood. We're rolling back toward our starting location now, but there's another name left to explore. After all, by the 1860's, South Bend had a population, a local government, stately homes, and a political star in Washington. There was only one thing missing:

Beer.

Christopher Muessel (pronounced like measle) purchased the land that would become the Muessel Brewery in 1860. His recipes and methods were traditionally German, and his early success was enough to expand operations, build neighborhoods for his employees, and later donate the land that would become Muessel Grove Park and Muessel School.[10] We used to make fun of that school because it was phonetically pronounced like a disease. Now that I know it's an elementary center named after a local microbrewery, I think it's probably the coolest school in the world.

Christopher Muessel incorporated his company in 1893, a year ahead of his death. He turned operations over to his sons and grandsons, and they continued to prosper, expanding operations in 1900 and 1911. Today, the maze of abandoned, condemned, and demolished buildings near Portage and Elwood represent all that is left of the Muessel Brewery. The company never truly recovered from Prohibition, was sold to another brewer called Drewry's, then sold again before operations were shuttered altogether. The buildings have been emptied since 1972 and whatever history might have been found inside has been stripped and destroyed. The city wants to raze it all and construct a new industrial park in its place. Among those interested in moving in is, poetically, a brewery.

We don't have to wait to wonder who South Bend's next influential father is going to be. Mayor Pete Buttigieg made a name for himself when he became the youngest mayor of a city of over 100,000 people in 2012. He made national headlines when he came out as gay in 2015, rose to national prominence with a Presidential

---

[10] Muessel Elementary School's mascot is the Cardinals. I find this to be wildly disappointing. Given the popularity of Muessel's brews, I'd suggest they change their mascot to reflect one of his beers. The Muessel Bavarians could be a fun name. The Muessel Silver Edge just sounds cool.

run in 2020, and then became the Transportation Secretary under President Biden. Before we roll back toward our starting spot, we jog across the river one more time to cruise by Mayor Pete's house and down the street he grew up on. As if he purchased his real estate with the symbolism in mind, Buttigieg's house sits just four houses down the street from the place Pierre Navarre's cabin originally stood; 200 years of history wrapped into a distance of about 400 feet.

We conclude our ride back at Pinhook Park, overlooking the portage where all of the old roads lead and where the history of South Bend began. LaSalle landed here. Navarre settled here. Coquillard and Taylor traded here. Chapin built here. Colfax politicked here. Muessel brewed here. Buttigieg made his name here. At its peak in the 1960s, more than 150,000 people lived here, and South Bend was one of the hundred largest cities in America.

All of that happened because this spot on this river was four miles away from another spot on another river. There may be debates about who the finders and founders of South Bend really were, but the answer is easier than all of that. It's right here at this spot, little more than a geographic curiosity, but the domino that set everything else into motion.

CHAPTER FOUR
A TALE OF THREE MISHAWAKAS

It's a chilly day in northern Indiana as we stand beneath the Main Street bridge in Mishawaka, surveying the grassy lot between the heavily trafficked street and the back end of Central Park. This lot used to be the site of the St. Joseph Iron Works and the St. Joseph Iron Works used to be the entire town. It would birth a community and spark the industrial operations that would spring up all around. Once upon a time, the place we're standing was in the middle of an expansive grid of manufacturing and industry, great brick buildings belching smoke into the air, the center of the town and its economy.

I remember when they finally demolished the place, watched on the news as all of it crumbled into dust. Now it's a destination, a beautiful walking path filled with cute restaurants and hip apartments. It's an incredible transformation for sure, but then, it's not the first time Mishawaka's risen from the ashes.

For all of the fanfare of its boisterous neighbor up the river, it was actually Mishawaka, not South Bend, that was incorporated first. It happened in 1832, twelve years after Pierre Navarre made himself the first white man to call St. Joseph County home. Alanson Hurd, a Detroit businessman, smelled opportunity on the river in the northern part of the newly formed Indiana. His prospectors had discovered deposits of bog iron along the swampy banks of the place that would come to be called Mishawaka.

The promise of profit would set everything into motion. By 1833, after less than a year, Hurd was constructing a massive blast furnace in Mishawaka, at exactly the spot that we're standing now, waiting to set out on a chilly bike ride through a typical October day in Indiana. Of course, massive blast furnaces required lots of workers. Workers needed things like homes and taverns and general stores and post offices.

So the town was born. A hundred men came to get to work on building the blast furnace. Capitalism took care of the rest. Recognizing the presence of several dozen lonely men, Earl Smith opened a tavern. Next came the general store. Alanson Hurd made himself the town's postmaster. Just like that, the town of St. Joseph Iron Works was a place with a population, an economy, and soon enough, a culture all its own.

We cruise in a wide circle around the parking lots, circling the furnace that would have been at the center of operations, the center of the creation of the town called Mishawaka. A moment later, we're rolling east around the Riverwalk. I used to come here with my wife to catch Pokémon. I don't play Pokémon anymore.

She's not my wife anymore either.

We cruise through Battell Park and I am choking back tears. I set out to explore St. Joseph County and I expected to explore the places I'd never been. It never occurred to me that I'd have to revisit the places I wanted to forget. I used to be happy here. I used to be so happy here. But the funny thing about loss is that even the happy memories will make you sad.

As much time as I used to spend here, I never fully appreciated the history of the place. Battell Park was once a platted town, intended as a separate settlement from the St. Joseph Iron Works, just on the other side of the river. They called it Indiana City and it was far from the only aspiring suburb that attached itself to the promise of the Iron Works. As many as five different towns existed within what is now Mishawaka's city limits, and as the Iron Works began to annex the villages and territories surrounding and beyond the furnace, it was apparent that the place would need a new name.

The choice was obvious. Mishawaka had been the name of the Indian village that stood here before Hurd showed up. Settlers adopted the term, referred to the rushing waters as Mishawaka Rapids. It seems likely that Mishawaka was a name already used in casual conversation when residents described their home.

There are two stories that explain the history of the name Mishawaka. The boring one is that the Native American word "Mishawaka" refers to the rushing waters that characterize this part of the river.

The more exciting story is that Mishawaka was a Native American Princess, the daughter of Chief Elkhart. The legend says that Princess Mishawaka fell in love with a white trapper named Deadshot. Their love was possibly forbidden. In an act of retribution, a Native American named Grey Wolf abducted Princess Mishawaka for his own, an act that may have set off a minor Indian war around the year 1800. It's a story that's been passed down, that the town claims as a part of its own story, and one that serious historians have cast no small amount of doubt upon. Either way, the town took the name Mishawaka and ever since, the place has been known as the Princess City.

Across Logan Street and back on the south side of the river, we pass the wastewater treatment plant, originally constructed in 1952, four years before a similar facility was built in South Bend. Mishawaka may feel like the kid sister of South Bend, but in this way, and many more, Mishawaka was actually first.

Mishawaka had the first bridge in the county. They also had the first dam. Mishawaka was also the first place to brew beer. We continue east along the river walk, dodging goose poop and pedestrians, then stop to survey what remains of the historic Kamm and Schellinger Brewery. The roots of this place run all the way back to 1853 and the great brick buildings that housed their operations are still standing. A tall smokestack soars into the sky, whispering the gravity of how important this place used to be. By 1900, they were producing 30,000 barrels of beer annually. But like Muessel and so many other breweries, Prohibition would prove too much to recover from. Kamm and Schellinger never returned to the levels of production it saw before the passage of the 18th Amendment. Operations were shuttered in 1951.

By the 1970s, the brewing district was transformed into a shopping and entertainment district called The 100 Center. It became the hottest draw in all of Michiana for the better part of a decade, but eventually commerce moved north and so did the customers. Businesses still stand in The 100 Center. A few even thrive, but much of the place is vacant. Significant parts of its historic buildings are in disrepair. A few weeks after the ride, the owners of The 100 Center would post it for sale, unable to keep up with renovations and the daily fines they incurred from the city for a failure to keep everything up to code.

But the area died and came back to life once before. It's not impossible to imagine that it could happen again. After all, reinvention and reincarnation are kind of what Mishawaka is known for.

The first time that Mishawaka came crumbling down, it wasn't on purpose. In 1872, Mishawaka caught fire. Despite the fact that the blast furnace at the center of the town was almost certainly a fire hazard, that's not what started the blaze. Instead the fire began in a barn behind the Presbyterian Church near the corner of Lincoln Way and Main Street. It was likely an act of arson that levelled the city, and the blaze burned out of control for days, ultimately destroying three city blocks and totaling 49 different buildings.

That's where we are now after dashing through a pair of stoplights and navigating a few sidewalks in downtown Mishawaka. We're at the place the fire started and where committed citizens decided to build it all over again. It was a turning point for the burgeoning city, and it's worth noting that the decision to save and rebuild Mishawaka wasn't an obvious one.

Already, iron deposits were dwindling in the area, and with the promises of the riches of the west, it must have been tempting for the St. Joseph Iron Works to accept its devastating loss and move into a more resource-rich area beyond the Mississippi. Such a move would have crippled the smoldering remains of the city.

But this wasn't just the St. Joseph Iron Works anymore. By 1872, Mishawaka had a population nearing 2,000. It was filled with churches and culture and families, people who had transformed the place into a home. Together they decided to clean up the mess. They rebuilt their city. The Iron Works stopped mining and smelting iron and started manufacturing with it. New industries would move into the revitalized Mishawaka and soon enough, there was more work than ever. Dodge Manufacturing would produce their Magic Jack Wagons for distribution across the Midwest. The Perkins Windmill and Axe Company built a pair of obvious goods just across the bridge from the place the Iron Works used to be.

Among the reconstructed buildings was a three-story brick building that would become Mishawaka's opera house, with seating for 1,000. The building was not without poetry; a sculpted Phoenix rising from the building's peak watched over a city reborn and remade. The building still stands today and is home to the Phoenix Bar & Grill.

Hints of Mishawaka's industrial past stand along the roadway. We see an old train depot, now used as a non-profit's business office. We cruise past the complex that was once the home to the Dodge Manufacturing Company from 1878 to 2006. Our route tosses us through downtown and then through a historical residential district. We turn south down Merrifield Street, named after George Merrifield. Merrifield was a failed gold speculator who would become among the first educators in Mishawaka and an elected member of the Indiana General Assembly. His bust is included in Mishawaka's Founders' Circle at the site where the Windmill and Axe Company used to stand.

From Merrifield Street, we'll ride out beyond the city and past George Wilson Park, where I used to sprint up grassy hills until I puked. It's a feeling I become reacquainted with a few moments later when an angry dog chases me over the top of a hill, nipping at my heels the entire way.

I breathe deeply once we're into the farmland and I regret it immediately. It's not the late 1800s anymore, and this is no longer the peppermint capital of America. As we cruise beyond the limits of the city and into the farmlands that surround it, the air is filled with the smell of fertilizer and exhaust. Traffic is heavy on the overpass today, tourists in town for Notre Dame football.

Peppermint farms dominated Mishawaka's agricultural industry at the turn of the century, and with more than 5,000 acres of crop, Mishawaka produced more peppermint per capita than anywhere else in the world. Put another way, that's enough peppermint to flavor 14 billion sticks of gum. It's said that during the peak of the harvesting season, the sweet smell of threshed mint would waft in the air and descend like a cloud over the city. For days, the air in downtown Mishawaka would smell and taste of peppermint, an impressive feat for a town that also featured industrial smokestacks and a high-volume brewery.

The Lebermuth Company would capitalize on the crop, beginning its operations by processing peppermint oil. For more than a century, Lebermuth has been an industry leader in the production of essential oils and has been headquartered out of St. Joseph County for the duration of its existence.

Not nearly as much of their raw product is coming out of Mishawaka today though. More traditional agriculture has taken hold in the fields we're riding through today, mostly corn and soybeans. Peppermint farms dot the landscape between here and Crumstown, announcing themselves with their smell from hundreds of yards away, but they are few and far between.

Mishawaka's farmland retreats a little more each year, steadily losing a battle to the expansion of the city. Our ride cuts through a new suburban medical complex, a place that used to be lined with farms and well beyond the reaches of Mishawaka's tendrils. It's not quite the city out here, but the city's coming closer, and Mishawaka's agricultural history is getting pushed further and further south, toward unincorporated communities like Woodland and Wyatt. Those places will be different destinations for a different ride on a different day. For now we're headed southwest toward the city, and for its part, the city seems to be headed our way as well.

By the time Mishawaka rolled into the 1900s, it was established as a regional hub of manufacturing and industry. There were plenty of jobs to fill, and at the same time, a wave of immigration was bringing plenty of workers to fill them. Hundreds of families would make the long journey to Mishawaka from Belgium and they'd settle the city's largest and most enduring ethnic neighborhood, a place called Belgian Town.

Today's Belgian Town still feels set apart, one of the few century-old ethnic communities that maintains a connection to its roots. Belgian flags fly over front doors and a crowd is gathered for Belgian bowling in the basement of the BK club. The architecture of the handful of buildings at the center of Belgian Town feels like a slice of miniaturized Europe. The West End Bakery still puts out the best donuts for miles.

At the center of it all stands St. Bavo's Catholic Church. By 1905, the Belgian community was deemed significant enough to support its own parish, and they chose Bavo of Ghent as their patron. To this day, it remains the only St. Bavo's church in North America. It's not certain how or why the first Belgian immigrants chose Mishawaka, but it's easy to see why they kept coming. This was a place that felt a little like home, and it seemed like Mishawaka was always hiring.

We roll east down 11th Street and somewhere along the way, Belgian Town gives way to one of the two distinct Italian neighborhoods within Mishawaka's city limits. A clan from southwest Italy would settle on the northside of the river. A group of northern Italians would settle here, on the southside of the river. A third Little Italy could be found in South Bend. Each enclave was settled by different groups of Italians from different parts of their mother country, and each group seemed far more aware of their cultural differences than their national similarities.

Today, rather than ornate churches in each community, the remains of Mishawaka's Italian neighborhoods encircle their own ethnic social clubs. Just a few blocks from the BK Club, we pause briefly outside the De Amici club, still in business after more than 100 years. Then it's back onto our bikes again, headed north through the city, toward the other Italian club that calls Mishawaka home.

*   *   *

Michael Portolese was born in 1896 in Calabria, a village in the southernmost reaches of Italy. He worked as a child, watching over flocks of sheep in their fields. He came to the United States when he was just twelve years old and got a job as a water boy working for the railroad. He enlisted to fight in World War 1, but the war came to an end before he was deployed. Portolese would return to Italy briefly before coming back to Mishawaka, returning with his new wife in tow.

He worked at Ball-Band and was active in the Italian community on the northside of the river. When a destitute member of the neighborhood died with no one even to attend his funeral, Michael Portolese called a meeting at his home and founded the DiLoreto Club. It was an Italian social club whose members promised to attend the funerals of all in the community. Today it's a members-only social club with a bar and seasonal events. I'm not a member of the club and I'm not Italian.

But I know someone who is.

A few weeks after the bike ride, I meet my friends Austin, Stephanie, and Greg at the DiLoreto Club. We drink beers and catch up on life. Austin, Stephanie and I have cycled across several states in the Midwest. Austin and I once bikepacked hilariously across Pennsylvania. It's been a few years since we've connected, and Austin shares photos of his newborn with me. Besides being a cyclist and a father, Austin is also a practicing surgeon in Hershey, Pennsylvania; the culmination of his family's American dream.

My friend's name is Dr. Austin Portolese and his great-grandfather was Michael, the same Italian sheepherder who came to the United States to work on the railroad and who founded the DiLoreto Club that still stands today.

The club and the neighborhood would make immigration safe and palatable for generations of new arrivals, but for as much as they came for comfort and community and heritage, it was always the promise of jobs that set everything else into motion.

Our ride points toward the expired Iron Works once again, and of course it does. Even after it ceased being the Iron Works, it was Alanson Hurd's factory building in center of town that kept everything else in orbit. The only difference was that, by 1900, there was a new man and a new industry that could claim to be at the center of Mishawaka.

Martin Beiger made his fortune in woolen manufacturing and his patent on a woolen boot is what put his company on the national map. He wrapped the tops of his boots with a black rubber band and a red rubber ball. The brandmark was a hit and Beiger's red rubber ball was essentially the Nike swoosh of its day. It was a marketing coup that allowed his Mishawaka Woolen Manufacturing Company to employ 2000 people in 1903.

As we continue on toward the place where Beiger's operations used to be, we roll past the Mishawaka courthouse. I can see the place where the factories used to be and I realize that those industries aren't the only things that have crumbled around here.

This is also where I finalized my divorce.

I am thrilled to turn away from the building and I catch myself pedaling faster, almost without meaning to. The sprint doesn't last long. There's something incredible to look at and it demands that we stop.

By the turn of the century, the Beigers were Mishawaka royalty and they were ready to build the house to prove it. Their mansion sits on Lincoln Way like a gate between the part of town where the businesses end and the homes begin. You can't miss it. At more than 21,000 square feet, it was obviously the largest home in town and if it were still used as a home, it would still be the largest home in Mishawaka today.

The drawings for the home were ambitious – 3 kitchens, 8 bedrooms, a bowling alley, and an ostentatious pipe organ among its features. It seems like it was a lot of house for the Beigers, especially considering they had no children. It seemed like a lot of house all over again when Martin Beiger passed away in September of 1903, just months after construction began. But his wife Susie was undeterred. She oversaw construction of what would become her massive single person residence, later travelling as far as Europe, Africa, Israel, and China to select furnishings for the home. Today, the Beiger Mansion is a bed-and-breakfast, but when it was still a full-time restaurant, the historic home was where Adam Driver had his first job, as a dishwasher in the kitchen.

Their home was a remarkable show of wealth, but it's worth noting that the Beigers still had enough money left over for philanthropy. They donated the money to build the original Beiger School, helped build the Mishawaka First United Methodist Church, and built and founded East United Methodist Church. After her death, Susie Beiger willed her mansion to be used to care for the elderly. Everything they built is still standing today except the business that provided their money. That would come down later and in a most spectacular fashion. But before the buildings would crumble to the ground, they would serve to forward another important part of Mishawaka's history.

After the treaties that brought an end to World War 2, the United States found itself faced with a new and unprecedented problem. The millions of men who had fought overseas were coming home. They were going to need jobs. They were also going to need places to live. G.I. neighborhoods sprung up all around the country, in places like the westside of South Bend and in a grid of neat homes just north of Mishawaka's downtown.

Normain Heights was built to accommodate more than 300 returning veterans as well as their families. The homes are understated, markedly similar, and impressively sturdy given the haste with which all of this was built.

It's a curious choice, but the roads are named after the most famous battles from the war and a set of decommissioned missiles form a monument at the center of the neighborhood. It's not hard to imagine a veteran, eager to forget the horrors he'd endured, living in a house on a road named after a place where so many of his brothers-in-arms were killed. Now that we're separated from the event, Normain Heights stands like a piece of history. It's where my grandparents live. It's where they've always lived as far as I'm concerned. I wave as I cruise past the house.

Homes for veterans were just half of the equation. They also needed jobs, and though Mishawaka's manufacturing renaissance was past its 1940s peak, there were lots of jobs available in the same places they'd always been. The Mishawaka Woolen Manufacturing Company had taken on the manufacturing of rubber products, then later been bought out by Uniroyal. By the 1950s, they were making tires and they employed more than 10,000 people to do it.

They made all of it in the same place where our car is parked now. For as much urban sprawl as Mishawaka has seen over the past 185 years, most of its life as a city has been centered around whatever industry was operating just on the south end of the river; first the Iron Works, later the Mishawaka Woolen Manufacturing Company, and Uniroyal after that. Each of these places was always the largest employer in Mishawaka, the driver of its economy.

That's why it was so devastating when operations were shut down forever in 1997. Mishawaka had been a chameleon with the times, adapting to different businesses and industries as they came and left: iron, beer, peppermint, wool, rubber, plastics. But they'd never been a city without a massive industrial manufacturing center in the heart of its downtown. All of a sudden, that was exactly what they were.

It was an unseasonably cold June day in the year 2000 when they pushed the button that would bring all of the buildings down. Thousands of people poured into town for the spectacle, the most who had gathered at the site since people came there to work. The earth shook. Clouds of dust filled the sky and covered the faces of the onlookers. And then, just like that, it was all gone, and the people were still left to wonder just what would happen next.

The AM General plant out on McKinley was promising, but with just 800 manufacturing jobs, it was a drop in the bucket compared to everything that had just been lost. It would take a lot more factories like that to fill the employment and revenue gap Uniroyal had left behind, and besides that, companies weren't calling. Without manufacturing at the center of its identity, what was Mishawaka now?

It would be an exaggeration to suggest that Mishawaka was set to rise from the ashes once again. After all, the city's third act was put into motion almost two decades before Uniroyal closed down.

The Mishawaka city limits are remarkably expansive, reaching as far north as Cleveland Road. Through the years, strip malls and shopping centers had popped up around Mishawaka, not far from its downtown, designed to serve the people who lived there.

By the 1970s, the writing was on the wall. The Uniroyal factory was aging into disrepair and the Uniroyal company was rapidly slipping from its place within the top 50 corporations in the United States. City leadership couldn't rely on the manufacturing that had always been its bread and butter, and to raise revenue, they couldn't rely on serving themselves anymore.

The new Mishawaka would have to become the retail hub of a five-county area, and that's exactly what happened. The University Park Mall was constructed in 1979, and during the next 40 years, nearly every single national retail giant had a home on Main or Grape Streets in Mishawaka. Piles of chain restaurants fill the miles-long gap between Granger and downtown Mishawaka. Parking lots are filled and traffic is overwhelming.

Despite the rich and long history of the county's first city, today Mishawaka is mostly known as the place people go to shop. That's a part of Mishawaka we can't visit today, at least not on bikes, because the roads are crowded and busy, filled with people getting a head start on Christmas shopping or refreshing their fall wardrobes. Anyway, I'm not as interested in telling the story of how St. Joseph County finally scored a Panda Express.

Instead, we pedal back toward the Riverwalk, the place where it all began. Alanson Hurd's surveyor wrote back that the deposits of bog iron around the river were virtually unlimited. He was wrong. Within twenty years the iron was gone and the reason for the city was extinguished. For the next 170 years, Mishawaka has swiveled quickly, adapted to impossible circumstances, reinvented itself overnight.

In a lot of ways, I realize that's what I'm trying to do too.

Our car is parked near the place where the Iron Works used to stand, but now its grounds are filled with luxury riverfront apartments and impeccably manicured parks. Young people walk dogs and skateboard around water features.

And yet, Mishawaka remembers and cares for its history. Once completed, the Iron Works Plaza will feature a restaurant and event center. The Red Ball Biergarten is an adorable summertime hangout. A replica of a Palmer Windmill stands watch over

Founders' Circle, where plaques remember and commemorate the founding fathers of Mishawaka.

Mishawaka has managed to move forward, beyond a set of circumstances that seemed bent to destroy it. They've remembered their past, but they've left it there as they've focused on whatever comes next.

I think it's time I do the same.

CHAPTER FIVE
THE DOCKED TAIL OF ST. JOSEPH COUNTY

It wasn't just the fur traders and iron workers that moved into St. Joseph County in the years following Indiana's statehood. It wasn't just South Bend and Mishawaka that were exploding. During the time between 1830 and 1860, thousands of pioneers helped settle dozens of communities that sought to take advantage of the county's most precious resource – rich soil and available land.

In particular, the land surrounding the Grand Kankakee Marsh featured some of the most nutrient-dense rich soil anywhere in the New World. They would have lacked the chemistry needed to describe it scientifically, but life-long farmers would have recognized the wealth in the dirt beneath their feet. It looked rich and felt rich. It smelled and tasted rich. It did not disappoint.

Our ride begins at the Phil St. Clair City Park, a stone's throw from the place where the Kankakee River used to be. A middle school bearing the name of Pierre Navarre is just across Sample Street. We stop to make sure our water bottles are filled. It's an oppressively hot day in northern Indiana, and we're not expecting to find much shade in our extended tour of western St. Joseph County's expansive corn fields.

We'd been here before, stopped briefly at the 7/11 where a portage used to be before we rolled west on Crumstown Highway. This time we're headed south along Mayflower Road toward a place called Sumption Prairie. Our ride becomes more and more rural by degrees until we find ourselves in the Indiana you've seen on postcards. By the time Mayflower Road gives way to Sumption Trail, the bustle of the city is reduced to a whisper and then vanishes altogether.

If Coquillard, Taylor, and Navarre were the first commercial pioneers in St. Joseph County, then George Sumption deserves credit for being the first agricultural one. He arrived here in 1830 and settled on the prairie that bears his name. It's tough to imagine it now, but for Sumption, this would have felt like an arrival in the promised land. His land skirted the edge of the Grand Kankakee Marsh and was dotted with a stream and a few small lakes. The soil was rich and thick, water was abundant, and best of all, he'd found himself a grassland prairie instead of a thick wood. Clearing the land for his crops would be so much easier. It was a secret too good to be kept, and by 1833, at least 20 families were living in the place called Sumption Prairie.

But all was not perfect in 1833. On January 13 of that same year, a pioneer settler named Isaac Rudduck died at the age of 21. The Sumption Prairie resident became the first recorded death in the county. George Sumption donated a chunk of his own land for the burial and the Sumption Prairie Cemetery would become the first cemetery in St. Joseph County.

I insist on searching the cemetery and I'm surprised at how well the old stones have been kept. It takes some doing, but I manage to track down Rudduck's grave and also the one belonging to George Sumption. I'd search out a few more, but it's a hot and windless day so we can't stay for too long. We need to move and begin to generate our own breeze.

How good was the land out here? In the decades after Sumption's death, his land would be purchased by James Oliver, the multimillionaire inventor of the Oliver Chilled Plow. By that time, Oliver had the technology to recognize the most fertile land and the wealth to buy it. He chose Sumption Prairie.

Barely seven miles from the heart of downtown South Bend and closer still to its ever-expanding limits, Sumption Prairie was probably too close to the city to develop much of an identity of its own. The historical record doesn't speak much of business development here and besides the cemetery, the only hint of history still standing is the Methodist church that opened its doors at the corner of Roosevelt and Orange all the way back in 1840.

Just like that, we're beyond the prairie, although there's no visual marker to indicate that. One farm flows into another, corn and soybeans, soybeans and corn. The heat is stifling. The road is baking. Salty beads of sweat sting my eyes and leave me pedaling through moments of near blindness. I can't recollect everything we saw during the next several miles, but most of it was corn. The corn looked healthy.

We skirt the edge of the state park and relish the shade of the thick trees that reach over the road. We dodge the northern end of North Liberty, a town with a story for another day. We find ourselves straddling the county line and we drop suddenly into Walkerton, a town with a fine history and an impressive record of protecting it.

* * *

By the second half of the 1800s, the fur trade was dead. Animals had been overhunted, the market had been oversaturated, and most importantly, fashion trends had shifted. What's more, there was another change happening at the same time. Railroads had become king. Aquatic travel along dinky rivers and meddlesome portages were no longer the most efficient way to get from one place to another.

Passenger and cargo trains crisscrossed the country, connecting major cities and major industries. But railroads didn't just connect towns. They created them.

Walkerton was platted by James Walker in 1856. Walker was a banker from nearby LaPorte and was the entrepreneur behind the Cincinnati, Peru, and Chicago railroad. The southwestern corner of St. Joseph County was a strategic midpoint between a pair of major cities and a logical place for a station. The only trouble was that there wasn't a town there.

So Walker built one.

The town of Walkerton dangles off of the southwest corner of St. Joseph County like an untied shoelace. A map of the county is roughly square, except that the spot that is Walkerton, hanging off the corner like a docked tail. It's uncertain why Walkerton was originally made a part of the county, but obvious why the county fought to keep it that way.

Walkerton is just five miles away from the town of North Liberty, and it's worth noting that North Liberty was there first. But during the first fifty years of Walkerton's history, it sat directly on the southern edge of the thickest part of the Grand Kankakee Marsh. Despite their proximity, during wet seasons, direct travel between Walkerton and North Liberty was virtually impossible.

In fact, the marsh served to separate Walkerton from most of the rest of the county. As we roll into town, it's obvious that something here is different from the rest of the towns we've seen so far.

We're not wrong to think that. In fact, Walkerton developed its architecture, style, and design separate of the rest of the towns in the county. Builders in North Liberty also worked in Lakeville and New Carlisle, for instance. There's a common feel that runs across the old buildings in those towns.

But builders couldn't easily get across the marsh. Walkerton was constructed by builders from neighboring counties; builders with their own styles and who were uninfluenced by buildings in greater St. Joseph County; buildings they hadn't seen. I'm not enough of an architecture buff to explain what's different about Walkerton, but a quick ride through its downtown does, in fact, feel different than a ride down the other Main Streets of the other small towns in St. Joseph County. Walkerton feels set apart. Even today, their library is separate from the larger county system.

Efforts were made on a few occasions to move Walkerton into a different county or to form a new county altogether, built from chunks of several neighboring jurisdictions. But St. Joseph County fought the efforts. They foresaw Walkerton's importance as a railroad depot and fought tooth and nail to keep it within their limits. They won.

During the next years, the New York Central, B&O, and Grand Trunk Railroads would establish in Walkerton, and for more than 100 years, Walkerton would count four stations within its borders. The promise of growth and wealth seemed guaranteed, but when the trains stopped stopping here, business slowed and industry closed. Walkerton would have to adopt an identity as an Indiana small town instead of a growing industrial center. The transition has not always been easy one. Downtown Walkerton is filled with traditional small-town trappings. We pass a few fast-food chains, some small business, and then the Firehouse Tap, possibly the oldest continuously operated bar in the entire county. It's not much. I've seen photos of Walkerton's glory days, but most of them have faded over time, and in a lot of ways, so has the town.

We stop at a Casey's General Station to replenish our empty bottles and something inside of my nose explodes. Maybe it's dehydration or maybe I've just smelled too much manure on the way to get here, but I am bleeding furiously from both nostrils. It lasts for maybe fifteen minutes before I fill up with a Gatorade and a Snickers bar and we decide to roll out once again. A month later, the convenience store will burn to the ground, a total loss.

The most famous of Walkerton's sons was Harold C. Urey, recipient of the 1934 Nobel Prize for Chemistry, and one of the fathers of the atomic bomb. It was a strange career path for a man who grew up attending Amish grade school and who was a religious pacifist at the outset of the war. Urey's impact in the science world would continue beyond the war. He would go on to attain a number of impressive professorships and was involved in the analysis of the first moon rock samples returned by Apollo 11. The middle school in Walkerton is named in his honor and Urey returned to his birthplace for the dedication ceremony.

We cycle past the school and then again toward downtown. Each turn feels like it will deliver us into a charming, bustling historic town center, but it never happens. There's a tension here, between those who cling to old, industrial dreams and those who see beyond the broken promise of the railroads. Old-timers lament the loss of large-production factories and advocate to just attract one or two big companies back to Walkerton. After all, it worked before. The more pragmatic view asks Walkerton to accept its lot and to embrace the small-town charms that could market it as a destination for vacationers and passers-through. As it stands now, downtown Walkerton appears to straddle the line between both and commits to neither.

That's a shame because the history of Walkerton is a fascinating one and thanks to the incredible Walkerton Historical Society, it's been protected as well as the history of any small town in the Midwest. A one room schoolhouse stands beyond the town's limits and the remnants of crucial train stations stand within. The mansion at the corner of Roosevelt and Ohio Streets is the largest home in the town and draws upon the glory days of the Central Cut Glass factory, once the crown jewel of Walkerton's industrial heyday.

But the piece of history I'm most interested in was found at a place that would become a Christmas Tree Farm, just north of downtown on Tyler Road. An ancient mound was discovered there, not unlike the mounds discovered in Lydick and in other parts of the Midwest. But this mound was of national interest and historians from as far afield as the Smithsonian descended upon the site with an immediate and pressing interest.

They discovered copper tools, weapons and armor. They also discovered eight skeletons, arranged in formation, "like the spokes of a wheel", according to a South Bend Tribune report. If the legends are to be believed, these skeletons were impressively tall, between seven and eight feet in height. Dozens of Indian tribes told stories and legends of an ancient race of giants. While theories about the genesis of these old bones abound, the fact is that Walkerton's protection of its history did not begin before 1922. The evidence is vanished, lost in geneticist's labs and maybe sold to traveling shows. Only a few axe heads remain in the custody of the Walkerton Historical Society.

We can feel the sun like a weight on our shoulders as we cross over and again the Yellow Bank Creek, once a tributary of the Kankakee; reduced now to a drainage ditch that feeds into another. The heat implores us not to explore a second antique schoolhouse and so we don't, continuing instead toward a community called Teegarden, a cluster of houses stacked neatly next to the place where a train depot used to be.

And then, once again, we find ourselves pedaling through infinite farmland, listening to hear if the heat is enough to pop the corn right off of the cob. I've taken to pouring water directly into the vents of my helmet. I should be drinking the water, but given the choice between dehydration and baking alive, I've chosen the former. We need another place to stop, but we are so entrenched in the middle of nowhere that it would take a miracle to find one.

But the Lord moves in mysterious ways and we don't find salvation at any of the number of pious country churches along the farm roads. Instead, we start to see the signs. We follow the arrows, and they take us to the most unexpected place of all.

Somehow we end up turning into the Calvert Rod & Gun Club for their annual corn roast. We're surprised to see this place, but not as surprised as they are to see us; a trio of sweating goblins in Lycra, teetering atop shiny bicycles with skinny tires.

Soon enough we're a part of the party. Everyone here is wearing every article of clothing that I've never worn in my life – camo gear and MAGA hats and football jerseys and shirts with pictures of ducks on them. The Johnny Cash cover band sets up their gear beneath a tailgating tent as the gruff lyrics of a certain Jonathan Mellencamp ring out from the PA system. A group of friendly hunters ply us with corn, soaked in butter, then drowned in salt. We take a cob and then another and another after that.

Listen, I was born in Indiana. I live in Indiana. I have never not lived in Indiana. I have a degree from Indiana University. But as I devoured a third ear of corn in a crowd of gun-toting, freedom-loving, Busch-Light-drinking, enthusiastic shooters-of-ducks, I realized something.

This was the most Indiana thing I'd ever done in my life.

CHAPTER SIX
A LAND OF FORGOTTEN PIONEERS

Our bikes bounce and jostle over some of the last sections of brick roads remaining in South Bend, and even though we are about 17 miles from North Liberty, it feels a century away.

We set off from Oliver Plow Court. James Oliver would make himself a few million dollars when he would invent the chilled plow and an additional 44 patents that made lives easier for farmers. The brick chimney of his old factory soars into the sky and still carries his name. Today we're riding from the place his plows were made and into the places they were used.

The near westside of South Bend is an area in decline, but it's an area that's attempting a rebound, and the thing about urban rebounds is that they don't happen quietly. They're engineered by the kinds of roaring trucks and screaming machinery that propagate the area the day we ride through, barely hidden behind a never-ending gauntlet of orange barrels.

Maybe there is no better way to appreciate the quaint and quiet charm of a place like North Liberty than to start from a place like this. At least that's what I tell myself as we rattle over one set of railroad tracks and then another. Our ride gives way to shipping yards filled with forgotten boxcars and a freight terminal abandoned by one trucking company after another before finding itself in state of disrepair deep enough to attract onlookers all its own.

All around, the air is thick with heat and the familiar soundtrack of the city in the summer. The drones of trains and trucks are punctuated by the percussive sounds of construction and destruction while the bumping of the rough road beneath provides the backbeat for the rhythm of a summer in South Bend.

We dive briefly through another neighborhood, once home to a Hungarian village. The Our Lady of Hungary Parish sits in the middle of the neighborhood, one of the few remaining hints of the place that used to be. There were bakeries and businesses here. The old theater at the corner of Indiana and Catalpa showed Hungarian movies into the 1940s.

Without the context of the history that tells the story of the place, these neighborhoods bleed one into the other, but each has its own heritage of culture and cuisine. If you use your imagination, maybe you can find it. As for today, the neighborhoods just feel like a construction zone because that's exactly what they are.

It's loud and it's pervasive and it interrupts every attempt at a conversation, but it doesn't last for long. The cacophony finds its decrescendo across Ewing Street on South Bend's South Side. Rum Village breathes the last gasps of the city, and then it's almost alarming how quickly the pace of South Bend gives way to the quiet on its other side. All of this used to be a Native American settlement, named after its tribe's chief, To Rum. The land would pass from the Indians to the Ewing family and then be sold to the city in 1916. Today it features disc golf, a high ropes course, and a mountain bike trail.

Four miles into the ride, a sign for a bike path beckons us into the Beverly D. Crone Restoration Area. The sign is a liar and the thing that it points to is not actually a bike path, but don't hold that against Mrs. Crone; the first female commissioner in St. Joseph County. Don't hold it against her eponymous Restoration Area either. This converted landfill has been transformed into a haven for more than 100 species of nesting birds including hawks, hummingbirds, woodpeckers, and even bald eagles. It's a feel-good story with roots in a more difficult truth.

Actually, it's a story that's not allowed to have any roots at all. The landfill was covered with one clay cap and then another. Vents were built to prevent the buildup of gasses that could compromise the caps. And for at least the next century, the Parks Department will have to maintain the area above the old dump to prevent the growth of trees. Trees have perseverant roots that could puncture the clay cap, something that would devastate the local environment.

It's a stark reminder that, like the efforts to restore the Grand Kankakee Marsh, it's almost impossible to fully put back together something that's been broken. Despite the best efforts and intentions, this place cannot be allowed to become what it used to be. The birds don't know that, though; so they've returned in impressive numbers, making the Restoration Area a part of the Indiana Birding Path.

It may be a good place for birds, but birds can fly and have no need for well-manicured bike paths. What begins as bad-looking gravel at the north end of the path somehow ends up even worse by the south end. We decide to leave the trail to the ornithologists. Following Linden Road to Johnson Road will get us to the same place anyway.

It's not Indiana without cornfields, and these begin just beyond the Restoration Area, growing tall enough in early August to block the crosswinds and to make it just a touch more difficult to see around intersections. But this is no worry. The traffic of the city has all but disappeared and the noise in the air has been replaced by a still quiet that hangs overhead like a cloud. If there are cars coming, they'll announce themselves among the silence.

The roads continue in this fashion for some time, long and flat, impossibly straight, only bending at those places where planners needed to accommodate a century-old farm that refused to sell. Further south still, South Bend dissolves into something more representative of Indiana on the whole with a blend of farms and forests straddling a perfectly laid grid of roads. Corn grows, cows moo, and horses gallop about their pastures.

It should have all been a perfect bucolic scene, but there was one unignorable issue. The fresh chip seal on the road was casting a pall on an otherwise excellent bike ride.

Chip seal roads are an abomination. They slow you down, dirty your bike, and turn your peaceful rural ride into a hand-numbing, crotch-rocking rumblefest. On a smart grid of roads, like the one we're riding today, it's usually best to go a mile out of the way in either direction to find a better road surface. But we can't do that today because we're travelling south on Mulberry Road and there's something important here, a piece of forgotten history that's worth remembering again.

The land would have looked so much different when Samuel Huggart arrived in 1834. All of this would have been thickly wooded, and the prospect of building a farmstead would have been daunting. Trees would have to be felled, their roots cut and pulled from the earth, every inch of the ground beneath Samuel's feet would need to be tilled and graded. Once all of that was completed, only then could he hope to deliver a crop. It was hard work and Samuel Huggart would have done it all by hand.

In the years before the Oregon Trail, Indiana was considered the wild west, and the people who settled here were no less brave than those who would cross the Mississippi and into the mountains beyond in the decades to come. This was pioneer country, and it was a difficult way to live. But for Samuel Huggart, it's not hard to imagine that he'd been through far worse.

That's because Huggart was a black man, born in Virginia, the son of a freed slave, likely a victim of some of the worst racism that the south could have legally doled out in the decades before the Civil War. By any account, he appears to be the first African American settler in St. Joseph County, certainly the first one to buy land.

Now marked by a faded historical marker on State Road 4, set too far back from the road for passing cars to take notice, the Huggart Settlement encompasses a full square mile, surrounded by Mulberry Road, Pierce Road, Oak Road, and Osborne Road. At its peak the Huggart Settlement included 28 individuals across several different families, all working together to tame and farm the land. The settlement would grow and thrive before, during, and after the Civil War; yet somehow, this was not the most amazing part of the story.

In the years after he purchased the land for $1.25 per acre, Samuel's brother, Andrew Huggart, would join him in farming the settlement. Andrew was the more outgoing of the two, and would quickly establish himself as a community leader, beyond the boundaries of the settlement, and more shockingly, beyond the boundaries of his skin color.

Andrew Huggart served on formal committees at the mostly white Sumption Prairie Baptist Church and was later selected as the superintendent of the Sunday School at Olive Branch. A full century before Brown vs. Board of Education, the Huggart children attended integrated schools in Olive Branch. Andrew Huggart was even permitted and selected to serve on a jury, the first black man to do so. At his death, Andrew Huggart's obituary was effusive with praise for his character and goodness. The South Bend Tribune noted that he was the first African American to run for office in St. Joseph County.

During the next several months, I would ask several people, including historians, activists, and local librarians what they knew about the Huggart Settlement. I was only ever met with blank stares. Somehow this piece of history was forgotten and lost. Somewhere within me, I developed a burden to bring it back.

Trouble is, there's not much left to find. The Huggarts and their descendants left their land to find work in the city for reasons that are lost to history. There's just a single log cabin that remains from the days when this was the Huggart Settlement, still used as a sugar shack for the making of maple syrup.

We jog east and then north and find ourselves on Millet Road, a road that is somewhere more rural than the others. It's the kind of road that connects nothing to nowhere, never part of the most efficient route between any two places. It's narrow and pinched like a long, fancy driveway. It's the kind of road you would never find without a reason to do so, and it's also the kind of road you would never have a reason to find.

That made it a perfect stop on the Underground Railroad.

Solomon Palmer was a white man and an outspoken abolitionist. He lived in the city, but he maintained a sawmill all the way down here on Millet Road, near the southern edge of the county. It's a hard business decision to defend. Even with a horse and carriage, it wouldn't be a terribly easy journey from Palmer's home in South Bend to his sawmill well south of town. With a headwind barreling in on us, it won't be easy for the three of us on our bicycles.

Of course, Palmer's sawmill was more than a tool to generate profit and its location was chosen for a different set of strategic reasons than its proximity to the trees. It was out here that he would aid and abet the escaped slaves who'd wandered off the more formal branches of the Underground Railroad.

A pair of major trunks of the Underground Railroad straddled St. Joseph County, one route through Goshen to the east; another through LaPorte to the west. South Bend's status as a quickly growing city made conductors wary, and there were only so many places to safely cross the river. Unfortunately for the conductors, the safe river crossings in St. Joseph County were always surrounded by a lot of eyes. Travelling on the outside of the county was safer, and it meant that the river wouldn't need to be crossed until Michigan, or maybe not at all.

But for a handful of travelers who got lost or who needed the most direct route to Cass County in Michigan, there was a smaller path that pointed through St. Joseph County. That path started here with Solomon Palmer and his sawmill. The place is gone now. It's been almost 200 years and whatever forest he processed through his sawmill has grown back in its place. It was in the middle of those woods where Solomon Palmer would discover the freed slaves who'd been sent his way, provide them a meal, and then transport them, under cover of darkness, all the way up to Niles, Michigan.

Thanks to the Fugitive Slave Act, it was illegal to assist escaped slaves, even in the north. By helping the fugitives, Palmer was tiptoeing a line that could have cost him his life. It would eventually cost him all of his wealth. Named as a defendant in the lost property case of Daniel Norris, Solomon Palmer's role in the South Bend Fugitive Trials would leave him broke and penniless, but not without his dignity and honor. He would go on to experience a financial recovery and would be elected to two terms as county sheriff. Not bad for a proud abolitionist during a time when that would have been a dirty word, even in the north.

Palmer's sawmill may have been deliberately placed in the nowhere parts of the new St. Joseph County, but he was far from alone on this slice of the map and he was far from alone in his ideals of freedom and justice for all. It's not even a mile from the sawmill to the borders of the Huggart Settlement. It's hard to imagine that their proximity is a coincidence.

It's highly likely that the Huggarts did not actually harbor escaped slaves as a stop on the Underground Railroad. Not unlike the justice system of today, the consequences for blacks caught breaking the law were far steeper. But their closeness to Palmer meant they could help in other ways, with food, materials, and even money.

It's hard to believe it today, but this little bit of agricultural limbo that hangs between the unincorporated parts of North Liberty and Lakeville was once a shining beacon of racial justice. It's a history that's been forgotten; and in parts of the rest St. Joseph County's story, it's an ideal that's been forgotten too.

State Road 4 connects the Huggart Settlement to the town of North Liberty. It's a highway and the shoulder is narrow, but traffic is light. The ride into town is not different than the ride down a country road, except that here, the road has paint on it.

*　　*　　*

The distance between South Bend and North Liberty is better measured in decibels than in miles. There's just fifteen of those miles between South Bend's city center and North Liberty's downtown, which bills itself as the 100th Main Street in Indiana.

Founded in 1837 after successful pioneer settlements took hold in the area as early as 1833, North Liberty peddles in a kind of generic nostalgia that doesn't bother to offer specifics. It sits like a town from the past, undecided if it belongs in the 1880s or the 1950s, certain only that it does not particularly want to deal in the present. Most of all, the draw seems to be that the town is quieter and more quaint than South Bend, its loud and hurried neighbor to the north.

We stop at a cute bakery for a muffin and a coffee and enjoy whatever it is that makes up the heart of downtown North Liberty. The town was platted by the Antrim brothers, an entrepreneurial pair from Sumption Prairie who dreamed of establishing a town with an identity all its own, far enough from South Bend to set its own separate course. It was a farmer's town at first and then sought to attract the attention of the railroads, but it was on the wrong side of the worst part of the marsh.

In the years before the Grand Kankakee Marsh was dredged and drained, North Liberty was too far south of South Bend for a rail line to go out of its way to reach it. But rail magnates coming from the south found the thickest part of the marsh difficult to build through and chose Walkerton as a more obvious intermediary location. Those realities continue to reverberate North Liberty to this day.

The railroads did come, in the years after the marsh was laid to waste, but it was too late. Walkerton had already been established as the more strategically important of the two towns. Bereft of the swampland that kept them separate and given the space of just five miles between them, it began to feel like there was not a need for both towns to exist. Eventually one would swallow the other.

By 1981, North Liberty was left with an impossible decision to make and they made it anyway. They seceded from the South Bend Community Schools, shuttered their own high school, and did something previously unthinkable. They sent their teenagers to Walkerton. It's hard to overstate the degree that a local high school

- 77 -

solidifies a community. It's hard to quantify the extent that losing one can decimate it. For the oldest of old-timers, it was blasphemy. They were sending their kids to the school on the other side of the swamp.

If the previous decades had spelled the decline of North Liberty, the loss of its high school should have been the nail in the coffin.

But it wasn't.

At the same time their community was being consolidated, the state of Indiana was at work on the creation of Potato Creek State Park. Just three miles east of North Liberty's main drag, Potato Creek would become a destination for travelers all over northern Indiana. It would become the thing that would keep North Liberty on the map. And none of it would have happened without the dogged persistence of Darcy Worster.

The founding of South Bend was a geographic inevitability. The laws of economics dictated that it would happen. If not Navarre, Coquillard, and Taylor; then someone else would have come. At Sumption Prairie, the soil was too rich and the land was too perfect. If not George Sumption, then another settler would have found it. There would have always been farms.

But a park at Potato Creek was never an inevitability. If not for the efforts of Darcy Worster and his constant botherings of the state government, there would have been no park, at least not here. Without the park, North Liberty might have vanished, its memories lost to Polaroids in shoe boxes stuffed into the forgotten attics of abandoned houses.

Darcy Worster was unceasing in his lobbying for the creation of a state park at Potato Creek. He folded paper to create origami insects, then mailed them with letters to the statehouse, his way of "bugging" the legislature to make a decision. Eventually, the bugging paid off; but Worster passed away before he could see his dream become a reality. Today the lake at the center of Potato Creek State Park bears his name and the place is a point of pride throughout St. Joseph County.

That's not to say that the founding of Potato Creek was without controversy. After all, people used to live there. A landowner scrawled a message on his barn before the thing was razed: "The Lord giveth, but the government taketh away." The government was unmoved and the project went forward. Anyway, this was once the site of an Indian village, so the farmer's message ignored another more obvious truth.

First the white people taketh away, then other white people taketh away from them. Either way, the park was founded and protected. Potato Creek would become a jewel of the area, and for the most part, North Liberty was back in business.

The park gained its name, Potato Creek, because the original pioneers saw the Natives foraging for a plant that looked like a potato. It wasn't a potato, but pioneers had a way of guessing at uncertainties and calling them truths. The moniker "Potato Creek" has stuck ever since.

We don't see any wild potatoes as we navigate our way through the bike paths in the park and down toward Lake Worster. We pause for a moment to watch the man's dream live on. Families swim and frolic on the beach, around the playground, and across miles of gorgeous hiking trails.

There's a cemetery within the bounds of the park. Several members of the Huggart clan are buried here alongside their white friends and neighbors, evidence of a forgotten racial harmony that would erode during the coming decades. Almost 200 years later, it's not certain that it's been restored.

There are big dreams for Potato Creek. Shortly after our ride, the state would announce plans to build an inn within the park and a bike path that would connect it to North Liberty. For those who own businesses in North Liberty, it's almost certainly a boon. For everyone else, it's a debate.

The prevailing feeling throughout North Liberty is that things were better in the good old days. There's a desire, spoken and unspoken, to return to those good old days. Problem is, there's not much of a consensus about when those were.

Some remember the heyday of the 1980's, when the local soda fountain was still open and when the bowling alley was always full, when North Liberty still had a familial identity. Others, remember the 1960s, in the years before their schools were consolidated, when storefronts would close so that the whole community could turn out for basketball games. The only book that tells a history of the town claims that North Liberty peaked in 1880. I'm dubious that those days will return.

Either way, North Liberty is left to contend with its desire to be a proud, tight-knit, and insular community while the state of Indiana does everything it can to help turn the town into a tourist destination. It's hard to believe that the money won't win.

I feel a kinship with the town of North Liberty. It's a place that experienced turmoil, pain, and desolation. It's a place that could have died, but it didn't.

It's a place that someone thought was worth saving.

At the same time, it's a place that has to contend with the difficult truth that even as it survives, it will never be what it used to be. Lives and relationships and towns are all things that change.

As we roll away from the gates of Potato Creek State Park, we find ourselves on a new road, this time skirting the western edge of the Huggart Settlement. Horses gallop in a field and I wonder if the people who live on the land even know who cleared it for them in the first place.

By the 1890s, the Huggart settlement was no more. Children and grandchildren were moving into urban centers, following some of the same roads into South Bend that we're following right now. We don't know why. Yes, their behavior was consistent with urban migration patterns all over the nation. Yes, more competitive agriculturalists combined with improvements in all kinds of farming technology meant that their square mile of land could only accommodate so many individuals before profit margins became so narrow that no one would survive.

But also, we know that racial attitudes were changing. Indiana passed legislation preventing the settlement of new African Americans in the state after 1851. Racism was being made law. The harmony of their predominantly white community may have been crumbling. Their place of honor among white peers may have disintegrated. They may have been longing for an acceptance that was no longer there.

We retrace the same path that took us to North Liberty, and like so many rural farmers, we're leaving it to come back into a city that's noisy and busy and bumpy and chaotic. As we dodge traffic and wait in lines at sketchy intersections, we're left to ponder the same thoughts as those who left North Liberty in the decades before us, the persistent question asked of progress.

The city doesn't necessarily seem better than the place we just came from, but it's too late to turn back now.

CHAPTER SEVEN
THE OTHER SIDE OF THE RIVER

The St. Joseph River has given rise to dozens of towns and cities, and although South Bend is the largest of these, it's far from the only story of settlement on the river's shores. Places outside of the county like Elkhart, Benton Harbor, Niles, and Three Rivers each have stories of their own to tell, and many of those stories also pass through St. Joseph County.

We're on the eastern edge of the county today at the place where the river flows across an invisible county line, bound for Mishawaka, South Bend, and eventually, Lake Michigan. But before the water rushes to any of those places, it passes through here, beneath the bridge on Bittersweet Road, where we're setting off from a library parking lot on a perfectly crisp fall day.

The river is at its widest here and the horizon offers views of beautiful waterfront homes. A handful of boats are on the water today, kicking up wake that ripples across the water before lapping gently at the shore. The speed limit on this road is 30 miles-per-hour, and as we pedal across the bridge, we're the only ones who aren't exceeding it. Everyone else is in a massive hurry to get where they're going. After all time is money, and money is Granger, Indiana.

Granger isn't a city. It's not even technically a town. Legally it's called a census-designated place, a distinction for places that only exist as ideas but have too many people to ignore. There are 30,000 of those people living within the ambiguous confines of Granger, Indiana. To put that into perspective, fewer than 6,000 live in the established towns of New Carlisle, North Liberty, and Walkerton combined.

Granger is a suburb and it comes with all the trappings of a suburb, sprawling subdivisions, strip malls, and a shiny high school that educates more students than North Liberty has people. Penn High School is the crown jewel of Granger, and when I was in high school, their football team would beat ours by 60 points every single year.

There's no great industry in Granger and the handful of farms that remain are increasingly bought by developers to create more room for more people to live. This isn't where the jobs are, and the people who live here are most likely to work in South Bend and buy things in Mishawaka anyway.

It's a fine place to live. It's where I live, in fact. But it doesn't have the most interesting history. First it was Harris Township, populated with grids of waterlogged farms and industrious pioneers. By 1880, the Grand Trunk Railroad planted a depot at the place the locals facetiously refer to as "Downtown Granger." It was either named after the farming organization called "The Grange" or Father Alexis Granger, a priest who ministered in the area during the years before a formal chapel was built.

Either way, the railroad named its station Granger, and the name of the community was set forever. A few businesses sprung up around the station, but Granger never became the center of any industry, and by all accounts, it never intended to. Instead, the next 140 years of the place's history involved razing farms, building houses, and developing an excellent school system. According to Wikipedia, Penn High School has churned out a number of high-profile alums including politicians, professional athletes, and one notorious murderer.

We're pedaling down Jefferson Road, skirting the southside of the high school's sprawling campus, the river just beyond the trees to our right. At the wrong time on a weekday, this road becomes an inescapable traffic jam, but on a quiet Saturday the road is smooth and the air is still enough for the sound of the river to whisper clearly to our ears.

By the time we reach Ash Road, we're at the eastern limit of St. Joseph County. The next county is Elkhart and this part of Elkhart is loud. Almost immediately we're confronted with the sounds of traffic. A car with a bad muffler turns onto the road behind us. He's coming from either the Wal-Mart or the Taco Bell and possibly both. The road ahead is already filled with the horns and rattle of trains. Baugo County Park sits in the middle of this never-ending cacophony, the eye of the storm, and the first thing you see when you officially cross into the town of Osceola.

Like so many things, the word Baugo is a bastardization of a Native American word. The tribes that lived here called the creek Baubaugo, which is literally translated, "Devil Water." Then, and now, Baugo Creek is prone to rising quickly and dangerously after rainfalls; its sudden rushing waters endangering game and crop along its shores.

The same waters also made Baugo an attractive spot for industry, and by 1833, William Ireland had dammed the river and built a sawmill that would harness its power. Just like that, Osceola was poised for growth and ready to explode, just like its neighbors to the west.

Situated at the place where Baugo Creek meets the St. Joseph and halfway between manufacturing hubs at Elkhart and South Bend, Osceola was ripe for development, ideal for industry and agricultural alike. But as we ride through the strip of pockmarked highway that best functions as Osceola's downtown, it's apparent that development never came.

Osceola is not a ghost town and there is no evidence of a forgotten heyday that's been left in a distant past. Osceola is not dotted with the empty shells of buildings that were abandoned along the way. Instead, it's a small town sandwiched in a narrow strip between the river and the busiest set of railroad tracks for miles.

We turn right, thankful to be off of the highway. We're into a neighborhood now, bound for a closer view of the river. Along the way, we pass the Pierre Moran Elementary School, named after a Potawatomi Indian Chief who used to call these lands home. Moran was a friend to whites and became fluent in English and French.

By 1830, as the last of fifty Indian treaties were being signed, the whites of Northern Indiana watched in suspense as the fury of the Native Americans began to boil over. Whispers of war filled the air. Wide-spread massacres were planned and promised. Only Chief Moran would stand in the way. His words and actions quelled the raging hearts of the region's first inhabitants, staved off a war, and saved countless white lives.

For his kindness, Chief Moran was repaid with orders to gather up his people so that they could be forcibly marched to Kansas. American soldiers on horseback would gallop behind and alongside the tribe, imploring them with violence to walk faster, often leaving the weakest ones for dead. The Potawatomi Trail of Death would kill more people than Chief Moran's peace treaty had saved. Moran would never again return to the place that had been his home. The students who attend the school named in his honor call themselves the Knights and their logo features a mascot of a white soldier riding a horse.

Further up the road, we're stopped at a place called Eagle Point and it becomes apparent what the white men would have seen when they chose to settle here. We can see where Baugo Creek spills into Baugo Bay and where the Bay rushes into the St. Joseph River. We spot an eagle soaring overhead. The place is not a misnomer.

The presence of two separate flowing waterways was a boon for industry. It meant they could dam up the creek to power their industry without impeding their ability to transport goods up and down the river. In the days before the railroads, this was the most obvious location for entrepreneurs to mill their goods and distribute them across the region.

But that never happened. It's less than a mile from Eagle Point before we've crossed beyond Osceola's town limits. For our troubles we've seen a sports bar, a strip mall, a bowling alley, a butcher shop, a school, and a church. Today, Osceola functions like an extension of the larger Granger/Mishawaka area, a place people pass through on the way to somewhere else. As a teenager in the 90s, I knew Osceola as the rumored headquarters of the Ku Klux Klan, a place where Klan Parades used to be an annual occurrence. I've made a deliberate decision not to name the man who claimed to be the High Grand Wizard and our ride will not take us past the farm where he bred hate.

In order to understand why Osceola never achieved the lofty promise of its bountiful resources, we continue west, back into Mishawaka, to the site of the burned down, rebuilt, and imploded St. Joseph Iron Works. Alanson Hurd got the place up and running in a hurry, mining and smelting iron with hundreds of laborers in the years when Osceola held just a dozen settlers. It was the wild west and water rights were scarcely understood and rarely enforced. The St. Joseph Iron Works dammed the river for their own benefit and when the locks broke, that meant the Iron Works was the end of the line. Boats could no longer get through.

It certainly wasn't in Hurd's best interest to fix the locks. Besides the outlay of cash needed to correct the damage, opening up the river would only make it easier for competitors to sneak into his market. The towns of Osceola and Elkhart sued the Iron Works, but their efforts were halted and stymied. Not willing to give up, Osceola set to the building of roads to connect them to larger markets. Jefferson and Vistula Roads were some of the first major roads on this side of the county, but by the time the roads were completed, the railroads were already on their way. When the railroads plotted their stations and depots, South Bend, Mishawaka, and Elkhart were considered destinations. Osceola was just a place in between them. It's a feel and notion that exists even today.

So Osceola gives way to a small bit of Granger which quickly becomes the eastern edge of Mishawaka. There are no signs that delineate these changes, no amount of rural land that stands between them. The raucous highway feels like one long city and the cars drive as if that's what it is.

The Twin Branch Area in Mishawaka forms the site of another dam along the St. Joseph River. Once upon a time, they harvested acres of river gravel from the shores nearest the dam. The first iterations of St. Joseph County's earliest roads came from the place where Twin Branch School now stands.

Further west, we navigate another set of Mishawaka neighborhoods, stopping briefly at a place called Monkey Island. No one knows how it got its name. There were never any monkeys here. We're stopped again a little later at the Shiojiri Garden, a Japanese rock garden that should feel out of place in the heart of Mishawaka, but somehow it seems to be exactly where it should be.

Dedicated in 1987, the garden celebrates the sister city relationship between Mishawaka and Shiojiri City in Nagano, Japan. The place feels legitimate, and it should. It was designed by Shoji Kanaoka, the same man who was hired as the landscape architect for the Japanese pavilion at Epcot.

I used to sit here in the midst of my deepest loneliness; the Tea House Pavilion the set of the fullest measure of my teenage angst and depression. It's poetic that I'm back here now, but the weather is cold and does not lend itself to sitting.

So we're off again, along the river and back through the heart of Mishawaka, past the place where Alanson Hurd allowed his dam to plug up the river and crippled the development of any town upstream that might try to challenge his own.

We navigate away from the river just for a few moments so that we can enjoy a brief cruise down Mishawaka's 4th Street. We're here to survey the Midway Tavern, now a regionally renowned blues bar. But during Prohibition, it was a bootlegger hideout. More notably, it was a favorite hangout of a certain Al Capone when he had cause to conduct "business" in northern Indiana.

At Logan Street, the boundaries of Mishawaka give way to South Bend, another unceremonious and unheralded transition in a never-ending urban sprawl. This neighborhood is called River Park, and it's filled with tightly packed streets and even more tightly packed homes. River Park is home to its own school and its own downtown. River Park carries all the trappings of the city including a city bus that squeezes us out of our bike lane. That's why it's hard to imagine that before Granger held subdivisions, River Park was South Bend's first suburb.

During the years before the urban swell of the cities, River Park existed in a quiet place between South Bend and Mishawaka. In fact, it was platted in 1900 as separate and independent town, intended as a well-to-do suburb. River Park had the best school and the most pristine churches. But as the cities grew, the margins between River Park and its noisy neighbors evaporated. The place had become absorbed by cities on both sides, and by 1911, just about a decade after it was created, River Park was swallowed by South Bend. It was one of the last successful annexations that the city was able to make.

As we move closer toward the heart of South Bend, we pass by IUSB, the historic Farmer's Market, the shell of the shuttered YMCA where I once learned how to swim, and a brewery called the Crooked Ewe that pours the best beers in town. All of this used to sit well beyond the limits of a city, but as its population expanded, so too did its borders. And as the American Dream became more about capitalistic success, the tastes of the wealthy shifted too. These were once considered the opulent homes and neighborhoods of the business class, but our route is dotted with modest houses in varying degrees of disrepair. What was considered large is not large enough anymore. What was considered exclusive is not exclusive enough either. The story of South Bend's suburbs is felt and seen here, five miles between the Granger that is and the River Park that used to be.

As populations left the city limits, moved further upstream and into the places where farmlands used to be, South Bend's population has suffered enormous decline. At the same time, the population of the larger metro area has swelled. More people than ever use South Bend's roads, amenities, and parks; but those things are supported by fewer taxpayers. The cost of suburban flight is felt throughout South Bend. The neighborhoods of UNITE and Edgewater are dotted with dilapidated houses, but not for neglect. They've been sitting empty, waiting for habitation or destruction.

Our route follows Northside Boulevard where the Notre Dame Crew Team makes its headquarters, but there are no boats on the water today. A few moments later, we're in Howard Park. Once a trading post for the Potawatomi Tribe, the land would become an eyesore of a dumping ground for years before it was cleaned up and formally dedicated as the city's first park in 1899. The addition of an electric fountain, donated by the Studebaker family, made the place the crown jewel of South Bend at the turn of the century.

Today, Howard Park features ice skating, playground equipment, beautiful views of the river, and a hip restaurant. The park is named in honor of Judge Timothy Howard, a local activist and politician who would go on to become chief justice of the Indiana Supreme Court. Of most import to me, Judge Timothy Howard would step down from the bench and become president of the Northern Indiana Historical Society. In 1907 he wrote an expansive book titled <u>A History of St. Joseph County, Indiana</u>, my primary source of research for every step of the adventures that would build the book you're reading right now.

A few years later, the city would add a second park, just a little further downriver and on the northside of downtown South Bend. Leeper Park, where I used to feed ducks and ride the curly slide, was christened in 1904 and once featured South Bend's first zoo.[11] Today it's a mixed-use park with lots of green space, a playground, and the new home of the Historic Studebaker Fountain that used to call Howard Park its home.

So Howard Park may not have its fountain anymore, but it's got something else that Leeper Park doesn't have: beer. The Howard Park Public House beckons us to stop for a pint, but our tour will

---

[11] When Potawatomi Zoo was opened in 1921, Leeper Park handed over its collection of wildlife. To this day, Potawatomi Zoo remains the oldest functioning zoo in the state of Indiana.

go on just a little bit further. In fact, from our vantage point along Jefferson Street, we can see the end.

The Century Center is situated at the spot where the St. Joseph River divides at the East Race. Originally, the race was dug so that a section of the river could be dammed and harnessed for energy while leaving the main waterway available for transportation.

Coquillard and Taylor were the first to claim the water rights at this junction, the race was dug in 1843 and then dammed in 1845. Ownership changed hands several times, eventually landing in the portfolio of the Oliver Chilled Plow Works in the early 1900s. The place that is now the Century Center used to be a massive hydroelectric power plant that provided electricity for the Oliver Opera House, Oliver Hotel, and several other Oliver buildings in the area.

But Oliver wouldn't last forever and other forms of electricity production would become more commonplace than hydropower. By the 1960s, the plant was defunct and South Bend was left with a decaying eyesore along the riverbank nearest its city center. They moved to fix the problem and they hired the best man for the job.

Phillip Johnson was among the most renowned architects of the 1970s, and the city footed the bill for one of his designs to adorn the site of the former power plant. Today's Century Center hosts more than 600 events per year, holds an art museum as well as an e-sports arena, and welcomes more than a quarter-million visitors every year. The views of the river from its Great Hall are poetic and stunning.

But we're not inside the Century Center. We're actually on the other side of the river gazing at the manmade rapids known as the East Race Waterway. As hydroelectric power fell out of favor, whispers began to spread about a new use for the historic race. By

1984, the East Race canal was reimagined and recreated as North America's first artificial whitewater course. Olympians trained on the waters of the St. Joseph, and today a tamer version is available to weekend warriors and tourists. A public art installation of River Lights entices nighttime visitors to linger at the water. I'm not pandering when I offer that the River Lights are stunning. Once the decrepit corpse of the Oliver power plant, this is an area that's improved so much in the past fifty years, even if other parts of South Bend have moved the other way during the same time period.

I'm struck as I think about Lathrop Taylor and Alexis Coquillard. What would they imagine if they could stand at the spot I'm standing now? What would they see in the city they once founded? And how would they feel when they found out that a lot of people were going out of their way to not live here?

The ride ends with beers at a place called The Lauber. It's a hip restaurant and bar filled with young and diverse people as well as a trio of dirty cyclists. I'm included in the latter group. Maybe our colorful clothes and pungent funk just add to the diversity.

JC Lauber was a survivor of the great Mishawaka fire of 1872. It was there that he learned to work in metal and there that he learned to persevere through impossible circumstances. By 1890 he had established the JC Lauber Sheet Metal Company, and his business would go on to specialize in metal roofs at places like the Palace Theater and LaSalle Hotel. Most notably, the firm was responsible for applying the original gold leaf to Notre Dame's iconic Golden Dome.

Not every piece of history needs to be bulldozed, obliterated, and built over. Sometimes the promise of the future can cling lovingly to the legacy of the past. At least that's what I think as a sip from my pint glass inside of an antique sheet metal factory. Soon enough, I'll put down my empty glass, load my bike into a car and drive back upstream to my home in Granger, where the bars are neatly scheduled into well-planned strip malls, without the messiness of a historical legacy to contend with.

Somehow it seems better to stay here. I order a second round.

CHAPTER EIGHT
THE WIDE SHADOW OF THE GOLDEN DOME

It's impossible to tell the story of St. Joseph County without also telling the story of the University of Notre Dame. Notre Dame's the single largest employer in the county, it's economic impact on the region is estimated at $2.4 billion dollars, and on football game days, Notre Dame's 1,200-acre campus will hold almost as many people as the entire population of South Bend.

But besides all of that, ever since Gus Dorais and Knute Rockne perfected the forward pass back in 1913; Notre Dame has been the landmark by which the rest of the country has known St. Joseph County. It's the answer we sigh when we tell someone where we live and they meet us with a blank stare.

"South Bend. That's where Notre Dame is."

For most of the rest of the continent, Notre Dame isn't just an important part of St. Joseph County; it's the only part of St. Joseph County they know. Knute Rockne, Lou Holtz, Joe Montana, Rudy, Touchdown Jesus, the Golden Dome, Lennay Kekua.

Given all of that, it would make sense if our ride started from outside the historic gates of Notre Dame Stadium, beneath a statue of Ara Parseghian. Instead, we're setting off from a rentable barn in the heart of Granger, the kind of place that hosts rustic weddings for suburban families. It's the easiest way to achieve the charm of an understated celebration while accommodating the pricetag of a gala. Like all of the historic barns that transformed into trendy wedding spots, this place started off as something different.

It started off as Notre Dame.

So did similar spots throughout Granger and throughout the county. During its first decades, Notre Dame was a fully self-sufficient university, even growing its own food at university-owned farms scattered throughout the county. The area that is now St. Patrick's Park used to be a Notre Dame farm. So did this wedding barn.

Today's Notre Dame carries the same desire for self-sufficiency, and in the past decade or so, has fought tooth and nail to build a bubble for itself within the county it calls home. An out-of-towner can attend a football game by driving in through Notre Dame's own exit off of the toll road, stay at hotels or inns on campus property, and dine at any number of restaurants within walking distance of the stadium.

Students attending the university can live four years of their life without ever stepping foot into South Bend proper. Many do. And who could blame them? For $60,000 a year, they have every right to expect the university to provide every single thing they could ever need.

We're pedaling west along Cleveland Road, alongside a handful of the farms that remain within Granger, not yet turned into subdivisions. The landscape is so very rural, at least for these few moments, and yet the area is not. Cars pack the road and crowd the shoulder. Cleveland Road in Granger, Indiana is the only place I have ever seen with traffic thick enough to warrant the need for a roundabout at an intersection that's bordered by farms on all four sides.

We jostle over a set of rough tracks and feel the landscape change around us as the cornfields give way to the neighborhoods and then into the edge of suburbia. Even here, Notre Dame casts a wide shadow and a heavy footprint. St. Pius is a massive church that has a strange obsession with cycling. They host group rides from their parking lot, and although I've never ridden with them intentionally, more than once I've encountered lost stragglers on the roads of southern Michigan and returned them to their parish.

St. Pius began at the wedding barn at St. Joe Farm; initially created as the St. Joe Farm Parish. But as the area grew, they needed more space for their people and their cars. Flattening good cropland was not an option, so they planted here, at a corner that would become a thoroughfare for commuters and the other travelers of suburban flight.

The next part of our route moves slowly as we cut through no fewer than six neighborhoods and subdivisions, jogging between paths and trails, dodging traffic and pedestrians along the way. A current Notre Dame student would never have cause to visit the white-bread cul-de-sacs of Granger; and yet you would never know it by the yards, marked with Notre Dame flags as if they were claimed territory. A family plays cornhole in their driveway on a set of custom-made blue-and-gold boards.

In all likelihood, almost none of these people are university alums. In fact, of the three of us on this bike ride, we've all spent money to wear Notre Dame apparel; and none of us ever attended the university. We're not even Catholics.

We pass through the parking lot of the place I work, a Methodist Church with Notre Dame roots. When the Indiana Conference of the United Methodist Church announced its intentions to set up a new congregation in the growing area of Clay Township, they began rallying to find a place to meet. The Catholics were receptive and so my roots run through Notre Dame too. The place that I've been employed for half of my life got its start in the engineering building on the campus of Notre Dame.

Our route carries us past Clay High School, a place that carries a South Bend address, but that sits comfortably outside the city limits. From there it's onto the place that used to be Clay Middle School; but it's been rebranded as the Clay International Academy. I only remember it as the place where we watched football games and marched through sleet during frozen halftime shows.

It's a few moments and a handful of stop signs before we confront the Dixie Highway and our next reminder of Notre Dame's reach into the community. Christ the King Catholic Church looms over the intersection, and when its school dismisses, it overwhelms the place for a few moments. Like many parishes in the area, Christ the King's roots run through Notre Dame. The $6500 needed to launch the parish were raised by Fr. Edward Finnegan, then the pastor of the Sacred Heart Parish at Notre Dame.

Despite the insular nature of its student body, it quickly becomes apparent that the university has fingers and influence all over the place. As we turn onto a bike path called the LaSalle Trail; we're about to learn that it's an influence that extends far beyond religion.

The path is new and the pavement is perfect, but its wings are overgrown. From our vantage point we can see the backs of the hotels that exist here primarily for one reason; to serve the population of people who are coming to visit Notre Dame. It's not just football either. Move-in weekends, graduations, academic symposiums, and alumni events are big business for the hotels and restaurants that have sprung up in the few miles north of Notre Dame. But it's not until we cross Cleveland Road that things start to get weird.

* * *

Roseland, Indiana is geographically a town within a town, surrounded on all sides by South Bend and then Notre Dame.

Economically, it exists to support the needs of Notre Dame. A census shows that only 630 people live in Roseland, and yet the place has eleven restaurants and four hotels. As for politics, Roseland is best described as the Florida of South Bend.

During a particularly turbulent time in 2007, town council meetings often turned contentious and occasionally violent. It was more than once that police were called in to quell a fracas and that arrests were made. Council members threw punches and threw chairs, all of this despite the fact that the council was made up of three people and that two of them were married to each other.

We jump off the path to ride past a Biggby Coffee, a gas station; and eventually the City Hall that oversaw so much chaos. The trappings of Notre Dame are everywhere, but this is not yet Notre Dame. Families wear hats and jerseys and I am sure that I spy a yard gnome dressed like a leprechaun and carrying a football. It's an impressive racket they've developed. Charge 8,000 students $60,000 to attend school for a year, and then convince the rest of us to spend a few hundred dollars apiece to adorn ourselves like we did.

It's so much different than how it all started during an especially cold winter in 1842. That's when Father Edward Sorin met with Alexis Coquillard in South Bend, then walked over to make official his acquisition of the land that would become the University of Notre Dame.

It was thanks to Chief Leopold Pokagon of the Potawatomi Band that these lands were already in the hands of the Catholic Church, but it was Father Sorin's insane confidence alone that would birth a university.

Sorin was dispatched to South Bend with three tasks: to run the mission that served the Native Americans, to administer to the white Catholic community in South Bend, and to start a college within two years. At his disposal was a swath of virgin land, a pair of log cabins, and the tidy sum of $370.

Somehow he was able to pull it off, and by 1843, they'd constructed the Old College, a two-story brick building that remains in use to this day. That makes it not only the oldest building at Notre Dame; but one of the oldest buildings throughout the county.

Our ride toward the Old College skirts the northwest side of the campus and takes us past the pond where my grandparents used to take me to feed the ducks. The area around Saint Joseph's and Saint Mary's Lakes was originally imagined as the heart of the campus, but now they sit at its edge. Any further west and we'll find ourselves riding through Holy Cross College or St. Mary's College, both still well within the census-designated place called Notre Dame.

The earliest years of Notre Dame's history were markedly difficult, and other than Old College, there's not much that remains from those early years. Fires in 1849 and 1855 burned down small parts of the college that had been built. Outbreaks of malaria, cholera, and typhus were common, leading to a pair of deaths in 1855.

But it seemed that no matter how quickly the university would fall down, there were always plenty of workers to build it back up again. As Notre Dame was growing in prominence and footprint, tens of thousands of Irish immigrants were fleeing their home country's infamous potato famine. Notre Dame would hire them by the hundreds to build the university, and Father Sorin himself would create a neighborhood for them to live in, a 120-acre lot south of campus once called Sorinsville. Later on, their neighborhood would be known as Little Dublin, and the echoes of the community's history live on through grids of historic street names.

Another wave of Irish immigration would create another Irish community on the west side of the river. This one was most often called Irishtown, and its residents were most likely to work in South Bend's industries and on the railroad, not for the university. Animosity ran thick between the two groups, and skirmishes and brawls were common, usually when the two groups would cross in the streets on the way to Sunday morning mass at nearby St. Joseph's.

It needs to be said that these incidents were in no way responsible for Notre Dame's decision to call itself the Fighting Irish. In fact, it wouldn't become the university's mascot until 1929. Prior to that, they competed as the Notre Dame Ramblers; and before that, they were simply the Notre Dame Catholics. In the 1870s; though, Notre Dame did not compete in collegiate sports and had no need for a mascot at all. By the end of that decade they'd have much bigger problems to worry about.

In April 1879, another fire would take down Notre Dame's Main Building, leaving no choice but for classes to be cancelled for the remainder of the term. Undeterred, they would build another one and this one would stand the test of time. Somehow the shell of the grandiose building was finished in time for classes to begin in the fall, but the building would not be truly finished until the summer of 1882.

That's when they added the iconic Golden Dome to the top of the Main Building; the most enduring symbol of Notre Dame, football notwithstanding. We dismount our bikes and gaze upon the Gothic building, bathed in sandy bricks, each window a poem. The place is inescapably breathtaking, and the history of its insides is even more impressive than the walls it shows to the world.

Notre Dame continued to grow and expand, eventually growing into a university with five colleges and a law school. Sorin continued to buy land to grow his operations, but there was one lot he didn't have that he couldn't get, not until after his friend Thomas Bulla had died.

Bulla was a Quaker in the middle of Catholic country, but he recognized something important here. He knew that Notre Dame was close enough to the city to be a part of it, and yet, it was set apart from the prying eyes that filled South Bend. To quote Scripture, it was in the world, but not of it. For Thomas Bulla, it was an ideal place for his station on the Underground Railroad.

Our ride pauses at Flanner Hall on the northside of Notre Dame's campus, a place once beyond the limits of the earliest version of the university. It was here that Thomas Bulla constructed his home. He harbored fugitives, fed them, and kept them until he could guarantee a safe passage across the state line.

Thomas Bulla's Quaker faith informed him of the evils of slavery and his devotion compelled him to fight against it. His next-door neighbor was none other than Father Sorin, and Bulla's clandestine actions did not escape the priest's sight. In fact, it was the common ground that became the basis of a lifelong friendship between the Quaker and the Catholic.

So Notre Dame was a growing university, a religious institution, and very nearly a harborer of fugitives. Beyond that, its programs were fairly well-regarded; and yet the school did not carry the national renown it has today. In 1915, Notre Dame enrolled barely more than 1,100 students; and was considered by most to be a small Catholic school somewhere in Indiana, if they'd heard of the place at all.

But all of that was about to change.

We're moving like pedestrians now, skateboarding our bikes through crowded sidewalks and past a number of historic trees. According to the St. Joseph County Tree Book; Notre Dame is home to many of the oldest and largest trees in the county. It's hard to tell which ones are the record holders, but even as we roll past them, the circumference of their trunks is obvious and daunting.

Of course, we didn't come here to see trees. We scoot to a stop at the place where this ride was always going to go, and we gaze up at the walls of Notre Dame Stadium, the house that Rockne built.

I didn't set out to tell a football story. In fact, I didn't want to. The history of Notre Dame Football is neither unknown nor undershared. But just as it's impossible to tell the story of St. Joseph County without telling the story of Notre Dame, it's impossible to tell the story of Notre Dame without telling the story of their football team.

That's because, for all of their academic excellence and for all of their wide-reaching religious impact; it was football that put Notre Dame on the map. When Knute Rockne and Gus Dorain spent a summer as lifeguards at Cedar Point, they spent their free time on the beach, running routes, playing catch, and inventing the modern passing game that's come to define American football.

It's not homerism to call their invention an inspired stroke of genius and it's not exaggeration to suggest that it changed the trajectory of the University of Notre Dame. In fact, it might have even changed the country.

During the early 1900s, there wasn't much pride associated with being Catholic and certainly not with being Irish. But when that small, Catholic school[12] from somewhere in Indiana marched out onto the national stage and started beating up schools like Army, Texas, and Stanford; a handful of marginalized groups suddenly had something to cheer for. Notre Dame became a national symbol, a

---

[12] It is not an exaggeration to call Notre Dame a small school, then or now. In 2021, Notre Dame's undergraduate population was a shade over 8,000; making it just the eighth largest college or university in Indiana.

rallying cry for Irish Catholics all over; not bad for a place founded by a French priest.

The impact of the feisty men from Notre Dame would extend beyond the gridiron and so would the challenges they were going to face. There were bigger problems in the world than Army's vaunted offense. By the 1920s, Notre Dame had made an enemy of the Ku Klux Klan, and the Klan was running the entire state.

We roll off away from the campus and toward the city of South Bend. We pass through a series of neighborhoods that function as an extension of the university, and then we're bound for the corner Michigan and Wayne. The new downtown library sits right here, and we arrive just days after the place has opened. The library is gorgeous and promises to serve hundreds of thousands of patrons every year, but we're not here to look at the library. This intersection was also once the site of one of John Dillinger's infamous bank robberies, but we're not here for that either. Instead, we're here to gaze up above the Thai restaurant and to remember when the Klan came to South Bend to start a fight.

* * *

D.C. Stephenson was a bigot, a racist, a rapist, a drunk, and at one point in time, the most powerful man in the State of Indiana. As the head of the Indiana Klan, he counted among his rolls one in every three white men in the state. He personally installed the governor, most of the Indianapolis City Council, several judges, and handfuls of state legislators. He relished his power and brandished it in horrifying ways. By 1922, the Indiana Klan was the largest in the nation.

Despite all of his successes, Stephenson had a glaring failure on his resume. He had continually failed to make inroads or to establish a significant presence in South Bend. If he'd been content to accept his losses, things might have turned out differently for him. But Stephenson's ego bade him try and in 1924, he made a decision he would later come to regret. The Indiana Klan was going to host its annual rally in South Bend.

It's a common misconception that the Ku Klux Klan existed only to oppress and terrorize African Americans. The truth is they existed *mostly* to oppress and terrorize African Americans, but their hate could be more widespread when it served their purposes. They spewed vitriol against Jews and Asians especially and sought to exploit the otherness of anyone who could be portrayed as a boogeyman. When they came to South Bend, they'd already chosen the targets of their hate. They were here to speak out against the Catholics and the Irish; and from the moment the Klansmen got off the train, the men of Notre Dame were waiting for them.

The Ku Klux Klan was coming for a fight. What they got instead was an ass-kicking. Notre Dame students challenged Klansmen in the streets, dragged them into alleys, punched their noses, and stole their robes. Klan members retreated into their headquarters at Michigan and Wayne, locked the doors behind them, and clambered to the third floor of the building that now holds the Cambodian Thai restaurant.

At the top of the building, the Klansmen erected a symbol of their hate, a tall wooden cross lined with red lightbulbs. The cross mocked the students below, and they schemed a way to destroy it. They ran across the street to a nearby grocery store and came back with a barrel filled with most Irish of all weapons:

Potatoes.

The students threw potatoes through the air, breaking windows and exploding red light bulbs one after the other. It took just a few minutes for all of the lightbulbs to shatter in a firework of sparks and bits of glass. At least all of the lightbulbs except for one. Try as they might, none of the students had the arm strength to reach the single lightbulb at the top of the cross.

They needed someone else.

They needed a quarterback.

From somewhere deep within the crowd, Harry Stuhldreher, quarterback of the Notre Dame football team, approached the barrel, selected a potato, and in a single toss, finished the job that the other students had started. Raucous cheers filled the street, and Notre Dame would win the battle for the day.

In the coming days, the Klan would organize an ambush of their own. They'd bring weapons and they'd overwhelm the students of Notre Dame. While the Catholic students were planning the third and most decisive battle, it would take Knute Rockne and Notre Dame President Father Walsh to calm the students and to broker a peace.

For the Klan, the peace came too late. Their ego and reputation had taken a beating, even as Notre Dame's was skyrocketing to new heights. They'd win a national championship less than a year later. Humiliated, the Klan began its decline in Indiana and across the nation.

As for D.C. Stephenson, he'd be convicted of a rape and a murder. The politicians he'd installed would be indicted for corruption. In 1923, the Indiana Klan had 250,000 members. By 1930, it was down to less than 4,000. The Klan was dead and the men of Notre Dame had a new moniker and a new mascot. From now on they would be called the Fighting Irish.

During the following decades, that famous Fighting Irish football team would attract a regional fanbase that included Protestants of all types across the Midwest, especially throughout Chicago. Their continued success would attract frontrunners and fair-weather fans. A 1991 national television contract with NBC would help indoctrinate a generation of fans from coast to coast. Movies like Rudy, legends like Joe Montana, and even the tragedy of Knute Rockne's premature death have only helped to further the mystique of Notre Dame football in the American conscience. And of course, like Irish blood and Catholic roots, Notre Dame fandom is largely genetic, passed from one generation to another across a century like an heirloom trinket.

The effect of all of this on the county can't be stated enough. A single home game brings $17 million dollars into St. Joseph County, and the impact of the 2020 Covid season devastated the local economy. It should have served as a wake-up call for the region. As thoughtful conversations continue about whether or not we should even play football, it feels inevitable that South Bend and the larger county will need to prepare for a day without the violent sport and without the massive revenues it brings in.

Two weeks after we rode through, Brian Kelly – the winningest coach in the history of the program – would leave his post without warning or notice; during a time when the Fighting Irish were still in the hunt for a national championship. The Golden Dome casts a wide shadow over St. Joseph County, and the uncertainty that was left hanging in the Notre Dame locker room would become palpable throughout the community.

* * *

No tour of the campus of Notre Dame is complete without a trip to the Grotto. We'll roll past the library and the basilica on the way there, each historic building standing like its own piece of art, brick and ivy and laden with rich history. But none of it is quite like the grotto. At night, this place is positively arresting. It takes your breath away. In the daylight the affect is muted, but it's still there. The place feels magical and spiritual. It smells like a miracle should feel. The prayers of the faithful permeate the rocks. And as for the reverence that hangs heavy in the air? Father Sorin would call that the Holy Spirit.

Notre Dame is a complicated place. It's lots of different things to a lot of different people. It's become a prayer pilgrimage for devout American Catholics and a kind of Disney World for the less devout ones. It's a prestigious research university, a tourist destination, and a football powerhouse; albeit one that leans more on its past than its present. It peddles in romance, nostalgia, religion, beauty, humility, and elitism all at the same time. Notre Dame is a successful university by any measure, but it's an even more successful brand. Its $12 billion endowment is the 11th largest at any university in the United States, despite the fact that it is dwarfed in enrollment by almost every school surrounding it on that list.

A bike path takes us west across Michigan Street, and although we're not on the campus of the University of Notre Dame, we still haven't left the place called Notre Dame, Indiana. Now we're cruising the campus of St. Mary's. Theologically and architecturally, it feels like an extension of Notre Dame, and in a lot of ways it is. Founded in 1844 and situated at its present site since 1855, St. Mary's was established as (and remains) an all-women's college. Given that Notre Dame did not admit female students until 1972, St. Mary's filled an incredibly important role in Catholic education across the Midwest. A lap of the 75-acre campus is completed in a few moments.

It's easy to dismiss St. Mary's as Notre Dame's little sister, but don't buy it. In 1970, when the two institutions discussed a merger, it was St. Mary's that shut down the conversation, not Notre Dame.

Our lap of St. Mary's complete, we find ourselves on another bike path, and this time we're pointed to another college, the third one within the confines of Notre Dame, Indiana.

Originally imagined in 1966 as a two-year institution for the education of Holy Cross Brothers, Holy Cross College is now a full-on college with more than 500 students and an impressive record in local mission. That having been said, it's most notable for being the place where Rudy began his collegiate career. The campus is small and unimpressive, lacking the historic charm and architecture of Notre Dame and St. Mary's. The ride around campus is little more than a tour of a parking lot and a view of the river from a vantage point I'd never seen before.

Then, just like that, we're across Michigan Street again, and headed back toward what is possibly the most historic part of Notre Dame; the Cedar Grove Cemetery. Of all the spaces and all the buildings on the campus of Notre Dame, it's actually the Cedar Grove Cemetery that was here first, even before Father Sorin took acquisition of the land.

Native Americans were buried here, at least the ones who'd converted through the work of the Catholic Indian mission. Alexis Coquillard is buried here. So is Pierre Navarre. Ara Parseghian and Regis Philbin are interred here along with dozens of football players and internationally known academics.

But there's one grave that's missing.

Knute Rockne isn't buried here.

When his plane crashed in Kansas, a tragedy that rocked Notre Dame and rocked the nation, his body was returned to his widow in South Bend. She had him buried in the Highland Cemetery, not more than a few of his famous forward passes from the place LaSalle discovered an ancient portage to the Kankakee River.

Notre Dame didn't happen by accident, but it didn't exactly happen on purpose either. It's the happenstance of the portage that made the place a settlement at all. It was the shrewdness of Leopold Pokagon that afforded a swath of land to the Catholics and it was the tenacity of its founders that the university never stayed burned down. But in the biggest stroke of fortunate coincidence, it was a Norwegian Lutheran named Knute Rockne who delivered Notre Dame to national prominence and international renown. It's tempting to chalk it all up to dumb luck, proof of the randomness of the universe. Father Sorin might beg to differ. He'd call it the benevolence of the Holy Spirit.

CHAPTER NINE
TITANS OF INDUSTRY

By the 1870s, the fur trade was dead. The economic engine that powered the portage and that attracted the men who would found South Bend had evaporated. As water travel fell out of favor, the place was, for the first time in centuries, no longer situated at a strategic crossroads.

But that wouldn't last for long.

Our ride begins on the gridiron of the place that used to be the College Football Hall of Fame. It's a mild day in October and the sidewalks are busy with people enjoying a day that feels to some like the beginning of fall, but only feels to me like the end of another perfect summer. It's a fairly standard downtown intersection at Washington and Michigan Streets, nestled between a pair of hotels and a fancy restaurant named after Pierre Navarre.

Only the historical marker next to a bank's parking lot belies the history of these roads. This intersection was the place where the Lincoln Highway crossed over the Dixie Highway; a pair of roads built to crisscross the entire country. The Lincoln connected New York to San Francisco. The Dixie linked Canada all the way to Miami. Just a few decades after the portage fell out of use, South Bend found itself once again at the center of the place where so many roads led.

*   *   *

It's hard to say what would have happened to South Bend if the Studebakers hadn't settled here in 1852. Probably it would have become home to another industry. Maybe it would have become a truer kind of college town like Bloomington or Lafayette. Possibly it would have ceded its importance to Mishawaka, where the Iron Works was already the single largest industry in the county.

But as the fur trade diminished, South Bend found itself at the top of the heap in a new industry, one poised to take advantage of the impressive roads that ran through all of the new towns on the map.

It's just a hundred yards into our ride that we pass through Jefferson Street, the site of the blacksmith shop that Clement and Henry Studebaker opened in 1852. They settled the place with a working capital of $68, and in their first year produced "two or three" of the covered wagons that would take pioneers into the west.

During the Civil War, the Studebakers provided wagons for the north. It was a hungry war, and the Studebakers found they could sell wagons as fast as they could build them. Operations expanded quickly, something that would prove fortuitous for South Bend on the whole. The fur trade had been drawing its final, shallow breaths for a while; but the Civil War was ultimately what killed it. The Studebakers were just in time to provide the city its new identity.

In 1856, Studebaker began manufacturing the horse-drawn carriages that would deliver its earliest fame. They manufactured high-top carriages for city tours, carriages for common folk, and gorgeous, stylish high-end carriages for the wealthy and influential. These were universally regarded as the Cadillacs of carriages. At least three Presidents chose Studebaker carriages, and many of those carriages rolled out from right here at the corner of Michigan and Jefferson.

By 1868, just 16 years after they opened the doors of their blacksmith shop with $68, the Studebakers had annual sales worth more than $350,000. South Bend was at the center of the world again. When an 1874 fire destroyed the plant, it was barely a blip on the radar of Studebaker's ascension.[13]

We turn south on Main Street, ride beyond Four Winds Field, and then under the bridge that's become a tent city for South Bend's homeless population. On the other side of that bridge, a handful of men huddle in the shadows of the old Studebaker Administration buildings.

It's in those buildings where leaders and knowers made the fateful decision to begin producing automobiles in 1902. We ride past the place where the factory was, the place where more than four million automobiles rolled off of production lines and onto roads across the country. Now it's all an empty field. The factory isn't there anymore. Its last remnants were demolished in 2013.

The presence of Studebaker meant an abundance of jobs and the abundance of jobs led to massive waves of immigration as well as the formation of dozens of neighborhoods and communities, often along ethnic lines. Poles, Hungarians, Italians, Germans, Irish, and Belgians were among those who came into St. Joseph County and who established their own enclaves.

But for the Greeks, who were among the last to arrive, there was little space for them to build their own place. Despite a population that would grow into the Great Depression, South Bend never had a Greektown or a Little Athens. Greeks scattered about the city and moved into established neighborhoods, ingratiating themselves within their new communities, but never losing site of their Greek roots.

Nicholas Prathaftakis was one of them, an immigrant from Crete who made a home in South Bend and built a life from the

---

[13] For those of you keeping score at home, that's three devastating fires during the 1870s. Mishawaka burned in 1872, Studebaker in 1874, and Notre Dame in 1879.

ground up. In 1900, just as Studebaker was deciding to produce automobiles, Greece was still considered a part of the Ottoman Empire. The Ottomans were crumbling and among the last tools at their disposal were the kinds of crippling taxes that left many Greeks looking for a fresh start. In February of 1912, Prathaftakis became one of them. He purchased a boat fare and set off for Ellis Island.

He'd later arrive in Dayton, Ohio; penniless and with command of just fifty English words. He spent his first nights sleeping beneath a bridge along the railroad. But the promise of America was not a falsehood. Prathaftakis would find work on the railroad, and he'd end up bouncing around the Midwest, working railroads in Toledo, Indianapolis, Chicago, and Gary. After a few raises, he was making $1.75 per day, six days a week, ten hours a day. By 1919, he was living in South Bend, selling from a cart along the outskirts of the Studebaker facility, and working as a cart-builder within the Greek community. He charged $10 per cart.

His hard work paid off a few years later, when he was able to put down a $300 deposit on a $4,000 parcel of land at the corner of Lafayette and Sample Streets, a place that would become the Paradise Restaurant. Today, the shuttered remains of the Dew Drop Inn sit where Prathaftakis's restaurant began.

I would have loved to try the special at the Paradise. I'd have even settled for a beer at the Dew Drop. Instead, I'd return to this place later to sit on the stoop of the shuttered building with my dear friend Lucas. Lucas is the great-grandson of Nicholas Prathaftakis, the man who used to operate a restaurant on the ground beneath our feet.

* * *

Today, all of this is known as the prison district. That's where we're riding now, into a fierce wind and along the layers of barbed wire that outline the confines of the jail. My friends and I are hollering over the whipping gusts of biting air, but none of us can understand the other. We're onto a bit of a diversion now, and we're not done with the Studebakers, but Clem and Henry were far from the only game in town. In fact, the soaring brick smokestack that pierces the skyline above Chapin Street carries a different name than the one that used to adorn cars and carriages.

We turn onto a road called Oliver Plow Court, once the site of the Oliver Chilled Plow Works, a place that was once among the largest producers of farm plows in the world.

James Oliver was born in Scotland, an immigrant who landed in Mishawaka by way of New York and LaGrange. He worked briefly at the Mishawaka Iron Works and made the most of his rapidly growing knowledge and expertise. By 1855, he was operating his own foundry in South Bend, but it was his ingenuity that was about to make him rich.

During his life James Oliver would register 45 different patents for improvements of the design of farm plows. Investment from the Studebakers would help the company grow and expand, and at its peak, Oliver was turning out as many as 300,000 plows each year. As his company continued to boom, Oliver would dam the east race to provide electricity to his businesses and properties. He'd purchase a grand home in South Bend and wire it for electricity, the first private residence in the county with such luxury.[14] But all of that was nothing compared to the luxury of his

---

[14] While looking for a place to park for this ride, we ended up parking at the South Bend Central Apartments. Unbeknownst to me at the time, it was exactly the site of Chess Mansion, James Oliver's home until his death in 1908. Somehow, James Oliver is only the second most famous man to spend appreciable time at this

son's home, and now we're headed down Washington Street to find it.

Washington Street has always been the most historic residential thoroughfare in South Bend. Frank Lloyd Wright designed a house on Washington. Almond Bugbee, the abolitionist who risked his life and lost his wealth to procure the freedom of others, had a boot shop on Washington Street. The historic home of John Bartlett is still standing. Bartlett opened the first bakery in South Bend and maintained his home as a stop along the Underground Railroad. The Civil Rights Heritage Center resides in the home of the former South Bend Natatorium. Once the largest indoor pool in the state, the Natatorium was the site of the longest and most contentious integration battle in the city. J. Chester and Elizabeth Allen fought to open the pool to African Americans. My middle school was named after Jesse Dickinson, another fierce advocate for equal rights who dove into the fray. Today, the shell of the former pool stands as a museum to their history.

But for all of its history, the crown jewel of Washington Street is the mansion of JD Oliver, Copshaholm. Located adjacent to the South Bend and Studebaker History Museums, the Oliver Mansion is truly magnificent. It features 38 rooms, 14 fireplaces, and contains nearly all of its original furnishings. Some of these furnishings were antiques when the Olivers moved in, including a trunk from the 1600s and a writing desk from the 1700s. There's also a secretary's desk that was once used by Abraham Lincoln, but

---

specific latitude and longitude. Before they were the South Bend Central Apartments, this was South Bend Central High School; and from 1934-1945, their basketball team was coached by none other than John Wooden. Wooden is arguably the greatest basketball coach of all time, leading UCLA to ten national championships in twelve seasons, including at one point, seven in a row.

that's only going to be the second most important Abraham Lincoln artifact in this chapter.

A tour of the home is a time capsule and so much of the place has been left untouched for decades. A bathrobe still hangs in a bathroom, a pair of shoes is waiting next to a bed. A closet in JD Oliver's den holds his collection of suits and hats. Bookshelves are filled to overflowing and the table remains set for a grand feast. A cabinet in the kitchen remains filled with aromatic spices.

The remainder of the grounds are expansive; a large carriage house with multiple rooms, gardens, an outdoor promenade, and, it must be said, more bird poop than I have ever seen anywhere in my entire life. Presumably, this was not a problem when JD Oliver still lived here.

The wealth of the Oliver family was a boon for South Bend. Besides providing for jobs at the Plow Works and building the neighborhood that would house their workers, the Olivers also built South Bend City Hall (demolished in 1970), the Oliver Opera House (demolished in 1978), and the Oliver Hotel (demolished in 1967 and now the site of Liberty Tower, the tallest building in St. Joseph County).

In arrears of the Oliver Mansion are a pair of connected museums celebrating the history of South Bend and the Studebakers. My kids report happily that the place is worth a visit. The Studebaker side of the complex features original wagons, sleighs, carriages, and even a few Oliver plows. Mint-condition Studebakers shine with the nostalgia of a sock hop. I ride bikes because I don't love cars, but I have to confess, many of these cars are beyond gorgeous. Besides all of that, you'll see record-setting cross country vehicles, the first car to break 170 miles per hour, and even the actual car used in the original Muppet movie.

But on the main floor, in the back of the room, is the most historic piece of equipment that Studebaker ever produced, one that has a curious story of its own. It's an elegant black carriage, and not long ago, it too was featured in a movie.

If you haven't seen Steven Spielberg's *Lincoln*, it's worth a watch. It's the most meticulously accurate telling of the life of Abraham Lincoln that's ever been produced. Spielberg's creative team scoured the nation looking for the actual artifacts from Abraham Lincoln's life so that they could include them exactly in the film. One of those artifacts is right here in South Bend.

Now, if you haven't seen the film, I won't spoil the ending for you; but right toward the very end, Abraham Lincoln decides to attend a play. For the short trip to the Ford Theater, he climbs into a carriage, specifically a Studebaker Barouche carriage; more specifically, the very same Studebaker Barouche that is a part of the Studebaker Museum's permanent collection.

When Steven Spielberg filmed the scene where Lincoln steps out of the carriage and the driver closes the door behind him, he needed a historically accurate sound. A crew came to the Studebaker Museum, set up thousands of dollars' worth of equipment and recorded the carriage door opening and closing. The sound you hear in the film is the very sound of the very carriage that Lincoln rode in on the fateful night that he saw that play.

Besides the collection of cars and carriages and the administration building, there is almost nothing left standing of Studebaker's industrial legacy. But the Studebakers were more than just carmakers and carriagebuilders; they were also residents of a city that they helped to build.

Just a few blocks from the Oliver Mansion stands Tippecanoe Place. Clem's desire to build the home is actually recorded, and he set out to build a new mansion, "one more nearly corresponding in its character with the position he had obtained in the affairs of the world." At 24,000 square feet, featuring 40 rooms and a staggering twenty fireplaces, Studebaker must have esteemed his position quite highly indeed. The South Bend Tribune reported that Tippecanoe Place surpassed every other home in all of Indiana at the time and although local press was prone to all types of hyperbole, this might have been the truth. The furnishings and art collections that adorned Clem's home cost at least half as much as the building of the thing.

Clement Studebaker's Tippecanoe Place is now home to a fancy restaurant and the Studebaker Brewing Company. The house isn't exactly like it was built to be, but over beers, I wander its hallways and rooms. A collection of children's toys and scale-model Studebaker wagons sits on a shelf outside the men's rooms. Print advertisements from Studebaker's heyday line the walls alongside framed newspapers and old photographs. The ornate woodwork carries a charm from a different time and a quick walk through the billiards room feels like a time machine. It's almost enough to transport you into another century, except that the Backstreet Boys are, for some reason, ever-present in the building's sound system.

Tippecanoe Place is at its most impressive from the outside. Ornate stonework and sprawling grounds begin to spell out the importance that Clement Studebaker felt for himself.

All of it is an opulent display of almost unimaginable riches, but to truly understand the scope of the Studebaker wealth, you have to look beyond their homes and even beyond their business. Today's ride will take us past places like Memorial Hospital, built with a $50,000 gift from Clem Studebaker. We ride up and down the city, dodging potholes and traffic, bouncing across antique brick roads, and then past the enormous building that once housed First Presbyterian Church, built by John Studebaker. Peter Studebaker built an Episcopalian Church that's now called the Cathedral of St. James. Jacob Studebaker contributed to the building of the since razed First Baptist Church.

But just like he did with his home, Clem would outdo his brothers when he built St. Paul's Methodist Memorial Church. The building soars high above the City Cemetery. Its architecture is ornate and classic. Despite its position on South Bend's westside, the place feels like it's been cast from a historic European city. The sanctuary features an extravagant pipe organ and German glassworks depicting Biblical scenes. True to form, Clem Studebaker himself makes a cameo in one of these glassworks. A secret network of tunnels is rumored to live in the church's basement, perhaps connecting the church to other downtown buildings, including his home, his daughter's home, and into what was once the First National Bank of South Bend.

A 2016 investigation into those tunnels was inconclusive and would have required tens of thousands of dollars to complete, although if the underground structures were intended to become tunnels that crisscrossed the city, it seems that the work went unfinished. We continue our ride, this time toward the South Bend City Cemetery, left to wonder about the undiscovered history somewhere below our wheels. It's in the rear of the cemetery that we discover the graves of the Studebakers, marked by the tallest stone in graveyard. I can't help but notice that Clem's not here. We'd find him later, marked with a modest stone in the Riverview Cemetery near the portage. It's poetic. If the portage is the thing that put South Bend on the map, then Clem Studebaker is the one who kept it there.

I've heard several stories about the demise of Studebaker. I've been told that they failed because their two-story assembly line was prone to breakdowns and extended downtime. I've heard that stubborn designers were slow to adapt to changing trends and that management was incompetent. It's been said that South Bend, a notoriously labor-friendly town, is responsible for the downfall of its chief industry. A popular narrative states that union laborers pushed for too much money and too many concessions, and that management was too eager to take care of their employees instead of their bottom line.

Each story feels like it exists to further an agenda, one that speaks out against governments or capital or labor. But at least one of those stories has to be true, and the most likely tale points to a severe mismanagement 30 years before its closure, a blow that Studebaker would never recover from.

Albert Erskine was Studebaker's president beginning in 1915, and business was booming during his first years. The company was called on to serve during the war, and they would dutifully comply, producing tens of thousands of wagons, water carts, ambulances, and wheels for gun carriages.

In the years after the war, Erskine found himself, much like Clem Studebaker did in years prior, with a desire to establish his own place in the company's history and in the greater conscience of South Bend. He named a model of a Studebaker car after himself, donated the funds to create the Erskine golf course, and penned a history of the Studebaker Company in 1919.

But the Great Depression was not good to Studebaker and Erskine's baffling decision to pay more than $11 million dollars in dividends in 1930 and 1931 would prove too much to bear. By 1932, Studebaker was deeply in debt and forced to default. Its shares now worthless, Studebaker ousted Erskine. Facing declining health, deeply in debt himself, and unable to face the failure of his time as president as well as the unpopularity of the car that bore his name, Albert Erskine committed suicide on July 1, 1933.

Studebaker would appear to rebound during the coming years, but it no longer had the resources to compete with the big boys. Their inability to invest in research and development might not have haunted them immediately, but it was at least a part of what would lead to the company's downfall in the years to come. Whatever the case, Studebaker shuttered operations in 1963, largely without warning; leaving a vacuum of 24,000 jobs missing in the center of the city.

In the 1950s, more than 150,000 people lived in South Bend; and Studebaker was its largest employer. During the next five decades, the population of South Bend would decline by a third – 50,000 people would leave the city in the next 50 years.

If it wasn't for Bendix, it probably would have been many more.

During the next miles of our ride, we'll pass both of the elementary schools I attended as well as my middle school. During those formative years, I never realized that South Bend's most important industrial hub was right between all of those places. But before we get there, we have to confront another truth about South Bend's place in the Industrial Revolution. For as much as we revere the heroes who became the titans of industry, we need to remember, they weren't always the good guys.

The city gives way to a place that feels despondent, a neighborhood called LaSalle Park. That's a relatively new name. It all used to be called, "The Lake." For a long time, The Lake was the only neighborhood in South Bend where African Americans were allowed to buy property. The place got its name because it was built around Beck's Lake, once a toxic dumping ground and now an EPA Superfund Site.

During the years when this kind of blatant racism was legal, it wasn't just homes that were hard to come by. Many factories, including Oliver and Singer wouldn't employ black people. Bendix would only capitulate to public pressure later in its tenure. Studebaker hired African Americans, but the record is mixed about whether or not they were treated fairly.

As for the lake, it's actually kind of pretty from a distance. It doesn't glow with a psychedelic phosphorescence and I don't see fish with legs or anything like that. But Bendix was dumping toxic waste here into the 1950s, a cocktail of chemicals that included asbestos, arsenic, and more.

The Bendix Corporation was founded in 1923 as a maker of brakes, carburetors, and starters. By 1929 they had an aviation division, and Vincent Bendix would decide to build something else. Bendix Field was the first airport in South Bend, little more than a dirt landing strip at first. Vincent Bendix's love of aviation helped spur continued development and improvement of aircraft. He hosted a transcontinental race every year from 1931 to 1962 and awarded the Bendix Trophy to its winners. Today, his landing strip has grown into the South Bend International Airport.

Vincent Bendix himself settled right into the role of an industrial juggernaut within South Bend. He purchased Elm Court, which was originally the mansion of Clement Studebaker II. He renamed the place Chateau Bendix and redesigned it in his own image, including a fountain that spouted champagne. During Prohibition he built a concealed area in the basement to hide his liquor. Today, Chateau Bendix is the site of Trinity School at Greenlawn, an independent Christian school east of downtown South Bend.

The ride along the former Bendix facility feels impossible. The manufacturing plant carries on forever, now filled with places like Honeywell and Bosch. Bendix brakes were once the gold standard, and while the stuff produced on the westside of South

Bend didn't make the world go round, it did stop it from crashing into other cars. But by the mid-1970s, their operations were already in decline. After a series of mergers, Bendix would later become part of Allied Signal and then Honeywell. What's left of Bendix today exists as a subsidiary of Knorr-Bremse, a German manufacturer of braking systems. The components that carry the Bendix name are manufactured in China.

The thirty years between the shuttering of Studebaker in South Bend and the demolition of Uniroyal in Mishawaka were among the most tumultuous in the history of the county. In the matter of just thirty years, St. Joseph County watched its three largest industries simply close their doors. First to go was Studebaker in 1966, Bendix in 1983, Uniroyal in 1997.[15]

For most of its history, South Bend was a blue-collar town, a proud bastion of labor with strong unions that fought for good jobs. But as the 80s gave way to the 90s, South Bend was a labor town with a sudden lack of industry. It's proved a tough hurdle to get over.

Our ride points through a strange and unexpected place, a final shrine to the legacy of the Studebaker and Bendix operations. We ride for miles, silently pushing strong winds, heads tucked low with Stoic expressions painted on our faces. We cruise through Lydick again, past churches and cornfields until we find ourselves on the western edge of the county at a place called Bendix Woods County Park.

Before the land out here belonged to the county, it belonged to Bendix. And before it was Bendix, it was the Studebaker proving grounds. Advertisements boasted that the land would become a

---

[15] The Oliver Plow Works closed in 1929, but given the rapid expansion of Studebaker and Bendix, the vast majority of its employees were quickly relocated, and the effect on the county was relatively minor as a result.

"million-dollar outdoor testing laboratory". It was well on its way, but the Great Depression stymied its advancements and then the mismanagement of Albert Erskine brought it screeching to a halt. Studebaker operated the proving grounds until it closed in 1963, but never had the cash to make the investment needed to realize its full potential.

Bendix would take over in 1966, and then in 1969, they'd donate 195 acres to the county for development as a park. Today, Bendix Woods features one of the best examples of an old growth forest in all of the county, maple syrup tapping, and chunks of an abandoned roller coaster, overgrown by greedy woods.

Most notably, Bendix Woods features a Guinness World Record that remembers the titans of industry who started everything here and throughout South Bend.

In 1938, with their limited capital, the Studebaker company planted 8,000 pine trees, arranged to spell out the word "STUDEBAKER." From our vantage point on the ground, it's not terribly impressive. But from the sky it's actually kind of neat. Go ahead, open Google Maps and search for Bendix Woods. It's still there, boasting to commuter planes, the world's largest living advertisement, just for a car brand that's nearly sixty years extinct.

We leave the park and all of a sudden we're headed back east. The headwind we'd been fighting all the way out here is pushing us from behind and we are flying, miles just melting away. We roll south on Tulip Road across the highway, and soon enough we're back into Crumstown, once the sight of the Studebaker's favorite hunting grounds. We're into roads we've ridden before, the roads that point to North Liberty and Walkerton. With the cool temperatures and the firm tailwind, I am lulled into something like a waking slumber, awash in a sense of peace that I only find on perfect roads on perfect days.

And then, out of nowhere, there is a castle.

We're on Chippewa Avenue, not far at all from downtown South Bend. I almost crash my bike when I complete both steps of my double-take. There is a full-on castle out here. I do not mean to imply that there is a very large house on Chippewa Avenue, and I do not use the term castle figuratively. It is a literal castle with a drawbridge and a moat.

I will spend the next several weeks researching this castle, only to find almost nothing about it anywhere, which is weird, because again, it is an actual castle almost within shouting distance of downtown South Bend. All I can find are a pair of unconfirmed and unsubstantiated urban legends.

First, that the castle belongs to rocker John Fogerty.

Second, that a jilted husband killed his wife, and built the castle on top of her in order to hide the body.

Neither one of these stories seems at all true, and today the castle is a private residence belonging to a private individual. I'd like to knock on the door and ask some questions, but there is a moat and drawbridge in my way.

Just a little further up the road, we pass another proving ground, this one belonging to AM General. If there is any business in the county that carries the legacy of the automotive giants who came before it, it's this one. AM General produces Humvees and other tactical military vehicles. Founded in 1971, there may have once been hope that AM General would fill a massive Studebaker-shaped void in the heart of South Bend. But today, AM General employs just 800 people throughout St. Joseph County, barely a fraction of what Studebaker employed at its peak.

What's next for industry here? I've heard plenty of old timers deride the local government, knowing that they hold the solutions to the city's problems.

"We just need us another Bendix or a Studebaker," they'll say. "We got the workers, just need to get the business to come back."

It's a desperate attempt to capture a set of good old days that aren't returning. There are no more Olivers, no more Studebakers, no more Bendixes. If there were, there'd be steep competition to woo them from every mid-size town in America; each one degrading itself more than the one before it to lure the promise of a future that could be yanked away at any minute, thanks to an era of outsourcing and conglomeratization.

As we return into the heart of the city, we roll past another famous building emblazoned with another famous name. The Morris Performing Arts Center is named in honor of Ella Morris, wife of South Bend financier Ernest Morris. Morris is responsible for leading the First National Bank of South Bend through the leanest part of the Great Depression. During the most difficult days, Morris gave half-a-million of his own dollars to keep the banks open and persuaded Vincent Bendix to do the same. Today, The First National Bank of South Bend has become 1st Source Bank, with branches as far afield as Kalamazoo and Lafayette. The Morris name remains written across South Bend. The Morris Inn at the University of Notre Dame was built upon his bequest, and the Morris Park Country Club was built out of his leadership. The Morrises would later become the owners of Tippecanoe Place as well.

It's not more than a block away from the Morris that we finish our ride at the same place we started it, the forgotten intersection of the Dixie and Lincoln Highways. Clem and Henry Studebaker would start an empire here, and their orbit would come to include Oliver, Bendix, Morris, and a host of other business and industry. All around, we see the town they helped to build and the town they rescued from the brink, sometimes directly from their own pocketbooks.

But that's not the way it works anymore. It's a lesson that South Bend's learned the hard way for the past fifty years. There's not an industrialist who's going to swoop in and chart the course of South Bend's future. That's something South Bend is going to have to do for itself.

CHAPTER TEN
DYNGUS DAY

As waves of ethnic Europeans immigrated to the United States into the 1900s, thousands of them would arrive in St. Joseph County to take advantage of the opportunity provided by the industry that sprung up along the river and the virgin farmland that was ripe for harvest. Often these groups would settle into homogenous communities all their own, each building their own histories and contributing to the larger history of the county.

At first this was entirely settled by Native Americans and would later become a thoroughfare for French fur traders. The first settlers of the county came from French and British roots and would quickly be joined by German and Irish immigrants looking for a new place to call home. Many of the Germans would settle northwest of South Bend, creating an agricultural enclave that would become known as German Township. Little Dublin, Irishtown, and Little Italy filled the spaces between Notre Dame and the southside of downtown South Bend. Mishawaka had a pair of Italian neighborhoods as well as its own Belgian Town. Later on, South Bend would see the development of Hungarian and Serbian neighborhoods on the city's southside. Reformed Jews filled in the spaces between South Bend and Mishawaka, in the areas nearest Potawatomi Park. Orthodox Jews settled in Twyckenham Hills, just south of downtown; and are among the most growing demographic in the city even today.

But most of all, there were the Poles. Of all of the groups that chose to build a home in St. Joseph County, it was perhaps the Polish immigrants who came in the most significant numbers and left the most indelible impact, especially on the landscape of the areas west of downtown South Bend. Polish Americans would build four distinct neighborhoods within South Bend, construct six Polish Catholic churches, and establish PNA clubs and Polish Falcons Societies to celebrate their heritage. They'd also leave South Bend with its own iteration of a Polish holiday that is celebrated almost nowhere else in the United States.

I'm talking, of course, about Dyngus Day.

Our ride starts from Casimir Pulaski Park on the westside, itself named after the great Polish hero of the American revolution. Pulaski was a Polish émigré who was made a general of the Continental Army after a set of heroic actions that saved the life of a certain George Washington. Pulaski is one of only eight people to be awarded an honorary United States citizenship. In South Bend, the park that bears his name sits at the intersection of what used to be three separate and distinct Polish neighborhoods.

As we roll down Walnut Street and across Western Avenue, we pass into a neighborhood now known as West Washington. But when these tightly packed lots were marked for their tightly packed houses, it was the neighborhood of Gniezno, a word that you almost certainly just pronounced incorrectly. This was where the first wave of Polish immigrants settled down in the 1860s, an attempt to start all over again, to build a new life in the new world, and to try to forget about the horrors they had left behind. Indiana wasn't exactly their home country, but then again, their home country hadn't existed for nearly seventy years either.

For decades, Poland had tried in vain to secure its independence from Russia and the January Uprising of 1863 was among its more dramatic and violent attempts to do so. It was not a successful effort and only served to awaken the anger of the Russian Empire. Decades of reprisals would cripple the Polish people, a stern warning to remain obedient. Hundreds of people were executed and tens of thousands were exiled or imprisoned. Properties were confiscated and burdensome taxes were levied as war indemnities. Left with no economy, no land, and no hope for a future; Poles were left with no choice but to leave the only home they'd ever known.

At the same time, industry was booming in South Bend. Studebaker and Oliver were ramping up operations. The Singer Sewing Machine Company was making a name for itself as well. Taken together, these three organizations would hire tens of thousands of workers during the next decades. For Polish immigrants who had nothing, South Bend became the place where they could step off a train and into a decent job.

Gniezno was the neighborhood in the center of it all, located equidistant from all three industrial hubs. Within a few years, their people had good jobs, a decent neighborhood, and a community to call its own. All that was left to do was build a church.

St. Hedwig's was the first Polish Catholic Church in South Bend. It was founded in 1877 and the oldest parts of its current building date back to 1881. The architecture of the place even feels Polish, like it's treading a stylistic line between European Catholic and Russian Orthodox churches. I've eaten a Polish feast in this church's basement, and when I couldn't understand the bickering of the women in the kitchen as I walked past, it's because they were speaking Polish to one another. Into the 1990s, St. Hedwig's still hosted a Mass in Polish once a month.

But St. Hedwig's isn't even the most ornate Catholic Church within a hundred yards of its own front doors. St. Patrick's was here first, founded by the Irish and German immigrants who arrived in the decades before the Poles. From the greater downtown area, St. Patrick's dominates the skyline. St. Hedwig's is concealed almost entirely in its shadow.

But for the Polish Americans who called this place home, none of that mattered. No longer were they borrowing a part of the city or the center of someone else's community. This place was all their own. St. Hedwig's would go on to found St. Joseph High School, now the dominant religious school in the county. And as for Gniezno, when it filled up, their population would spill over into another neighborhood, today called simply the Westside.

We cross back over Western Avenue and into a neighborhood once called "Warszawa", the second Polish neighborhood that would come to dominate this side of the city. By 1898, the area was populated enough to warrant a second parish. Just twelve years after Gniezno built St. Hedwig's, Warszawa would build St. Casimir's.

St. Casimir is not related to Casimir Pulaski. He lived about 300 years earlier, and even though he was born in Poland, he did his most notable works throughout Lithuania. Today, St. Casimir is the patron saint of Lithuania and Lithuanian youth. The church in South Bend that's named in his honor isn't stunning on the outside. In fact, it's faded like a piece of history that disappears into the community around it. But trust me, this place is gorgeous on the inside. The Historic Preservation Commission gives St. Casimir's a perfect score: thirteen out of thirteen.[16]

It would be easy enough to stay in this part of the city. It would certainly be an easier ride, and with temperatures topping out in the mid-40s, it's tempting to make it a short one. There's certainly enough history here to fill several pages. By 1912, these Polish neighborhoods had more than 30 grocery stores all their own, in addition to butcher shoppes, bakeries, and more than a half-dozen tailors.

---

[16] Yes, that is a silly way to rate things.

But the Polish history of St. Joseph County extends beyond the westside and into the places west of South Bend. Not every Polish immigrant wanted to work in a factory forever. In fact, several of them pinched pennies and saved money, long enough to buy a tract of land they could call their own. In the years after they immigrated to South Bend, there was a second Polish migration. Poles from the city were moving to the country and they would begin their own community somewhere southwest of the place that would become Lydick, Indiana.

As we ride west out of South Bend, I find myself surprised to be on the same set of roads that so many of these rides have taken me through during the past ten chapters. I'd never seen Lydick in my life, and yet here we are again, passing through the place that functions as its downtown. I'm sure this church parking lot is always empty, but someone is ringing bells in there. As soon as I try to comprehend it, Lydick is over and we're back into the country.

Cattle huddle in a field and I huddle in the draft to beat the cold even more than I beat the wind. My nose is running, but it freezes into crystals before it can drip. I tuck my head and put on a brave face. Soon enough we're at the next stop on our tour of the Polish history of St. Joseph County. It's too cold to pause for long, but here's the St. Stanislaus Kostka Parish, established during the years between Hedwig and Casimir.

Terre Coupee sits in the area between Lydick and New Carlisle. Geologically, the land was prairie, stock with rich soil, just begging for industrious farmers to take advantage of it. A handful of Polish families, among the first to relocate to Indiana, saved up money and purchased land in the country. Their land would be passed down through family lines, sold and then sold again, but in this part of the county, it remains agricultural land. Hints of their farms and the boundaries of their lands still remains.

At St. Stanislaus, their heritage remains as well. This was actually the second Polish parish in the area, founded even before St. Casimir. The faithful farmers made every attempt to get back to the city for worship, but inclement weather often made that an impossibility. It shouldn't be surprising. The French translation of Terre Coupee literally means "cut off." Recognizing this, Father Valentine Czyzewski, then the pastor at St. Hedwig and undoubtedly the most important figure in South Bend's Polish history, authorized the creation of the new parish at Terre Coupee.

Among other things, Stanislaus Kostka is venerated as the patron saint of broken bones. At his death, Kostka was just 17 years old, making him one of the youngest saints of the Catholic Church. It was a choice that Czyzewski made on purpose as the community he was planting was as youthful and new as the child saint that would give his name to the place.

Czyzewski would visit the name again when he planted a third parish within the bounds of South Bend. St. Stan's in the Near Northwest neighborhood would become the third of its kind in the city and today, it's the most traditional of all, a personal parish with Latin masses steeped in the oldest customs.

Even now, Terre Coupee retains much of its Polish heritage. Just south of the parish, we ride past the last PNA in St. Joseph County. I used to bowl at a similar club in South Bend, but it has since been closed and demolished. Polish social clubs still exist throughout the county. Besides the Polish National Alliance out here, there are a pair of Falcon Clubs in the city. They're all pretty similar. A small membership fee grants you access to a cash bar, hall rentals, a few pool tables, and seasonal events.

In St. Joseph County, there's only one seasonal event that matters, and as we push the headwind back into the city of South

Bend, I realize it's going to take the rest of our ride for me to explain it.

For Catholics, the season of Lent is a big deal and the celebration of Easter is an even bigger one. I'm not sure if any of it is a bigger deal for Polish Catholics, but I can tell you with certainty that if they don't celebrate in a bigger way, they definitely celebrate in a different way.

Fat Tuesday is a holiday all over the world. In New Orleans, people get drunk, women take off their shirts, and people throw beads. It's a last hurrah before the sacrifices that define the Lenten season, just as Jesus would have wanted. In South Bend, we celebrate differently, in a way that is distinctly Polish.

Lenten restrictions could wipe out entire bakeries throughout Poland. Sugar, lard, and preserves were all considered among the things that a faithful Catholic would give up for the duration of Lent. Polish bakers, afraid that their supplies would spoil during the 40 days of waiting, invented a new pastry, one that would allow them to use up every ounce of the unhealthy ingredients in their pantry. They invented the pączki.[17]

A pączki is essentially a massive jelly-filled donut covered in sugar that, for some reason, is also made with grain alcohol. It is truly a baker's attempt to use up every forboden ingredient before Ash Wednesday, the first day of Lent. Inevitably, someone will bring a few dozen of these sugar-packed carb-bombs into any South Bend office building on Fat Tuesday. It's like Russian Roulette choosing one from the box, and you cross your fingers, hoping you didn't choose the one filled with prunes. By 11:00 in the morning, you and all of your coworkers need a nap.

---

[17] Don't feel bad if you don't know how to pronounce that word. I've lived here most of my life, I've heard it pronounced at least four different ways, and I have no idea which one is correct.

Once upon a time, my very German grandma happened to stop by her favorite bakery on a Fat Tuesday, unaware of the Polish tradition that was well underway. For reasons unbeknownst to her, the line for the bakery stretched around the block. For reasons unbeknownst to me, she waited in the line anyway. A reporter with a local news station accosted my grandmother, shoved a microphone in her face, and asked how many pączkis she was going to purchase.

"Pączkis?" she responded. "What is a pączki? I'm here to buy a loaf of pumpernickel rye bread!"

I share this story with my friends as we pedal into a block headwind. The wind is loud and I don't know how much of the story they even heard. But that's okay, because the most Polish of celebrations isn't actually about how they start the season of Lent. It's how they end it.

Dyngus Day is the Monday after Easter. It's the blowout party after all of the Lenten restrictions have ended. For devout Polish Catholics, it marks the end of a month-and-a-half of vegetarianism and sobriety. For the rest of us, we're just glad to be invited to the party.

At Polish Catholic churches, at the PNA, at the Falcon's Club, and even at the occasional fancy bowling alley, Dyngus Day means Polish sausage, noodles, potatoes, green beans, fried chicken, and an endless supply of cheap draft beer. In South Bend, it literally means the beginning of the political campaign season. Robert Kennedy, Bill Clinton, and Barack Obama are among those who have campaigned in South Bend on Dyngus Day.

Despite the fact that its very name sounds like a thing made up by a child, Dyngus Day is a very real thing. At once, it is a religious holiday, an ethnic holiday, a political holiday, and a tailgate.

I know, it sounds like a weird thing, but I assure you, it comes from weirder roots

Traditionally celebrated in Poland, Dyngus Day often involves boys dressed as bears, soaking girls with water, and spanking their bottoms with something called a pussy willow. Sometimes, boys would break into a girl's home, and toss her into lake. Sometimes they'd toss her into a lake along with her bed. In fairness, the girls were allowed to take their revenge on Tuesday. For what it's worth, I've looked into it, and none of this seems to be scriptural. But with all of that taken into account, suddenly South Bend's version of Dyngus Day doesn't seem so odd.

By the time I finish telling the story of Dyngus Day, we're past the Chamberlain Lake Nature Preserve, through Sumption Prairie, and back within the city limits. Our ride feels like it should be nearing its finish, but there's still one more neighborhood, a pair of churches, and a whole host of drama left to unpack before we can get back to the car.

The Krakow neighborhood encompassed the westside of the Westside and by 1905, the place was filled with enough Poles to warrant construction of yet another ethnically Polish Catholic Church, the fifth in the county, and the fourth within a narrow slice of South Bend's city limits.

St. Adalbert is known as the patron saint of Prague, but he died in Poland; and so the fifth Polish parish in the region took his name as their own. Krakow founded the parish in 1905 and constructed their current building in 1926, but in between is when all the excitement happened.

Given that there were four ethnically Polish parishes within a mile or two of one another, there was bound to be some amount of conflict between them. In 1913, a new priest at St. Adalbert's vehemently opposed the use of alcohol. Unfortunately for him, his congregation was Polish.

The controversy would lead to the founding of yet another congregation on this side of town, the St. Mary's Polish National Catholic Church, the starkest and plainest brick building of all of them. Tensions ran high between those loyal to St. Adalbert's and those who defected to St. Mary's, now the sixth ethnically Polish church on this side of the county.

But that was nothing compared to the drama just down the street at St. Casimir's. In 1914, a controversial new pastoral appointment incited a riot, and not a small one. When the new pastor attempted to take the pulpit, a throng of 1,000 angry Polish Catholics opposed him. When police officers were dispatched to quell the fracas, they were quickly overwhelmed by the rioters, on account of there were a thousand of them. In the end, 23 people were arrested.

Our ride carries us back toward Pulaski Park and asks us to notice the changing neighborhoods around us. There are still hints of Polish architecture lining the street, and brick buildings whisper towards a distant past, but Poles don't dominate the scene here anymore. The historic parishes offer as many masses in Spanish as they do English. Western Avenue is bereft of the Polish bakeries that used to line the roadway; instead the place is filled with taquerias and the smell is intoxicating.

These neighborhoods have lost their names and gained new identities. By the mid-1900s, the Poles were beginning to move out. Jobs were diminishing and there were opportunities elsewhere. In their place came African Americans; part of a Great Migration from the Jim Crow South. It wouldn't be until the 1950s that African Americans outnumbered the foreign-born population of South Bend.

By the 1990s, those same neighborhoods gave way to the significant Hispanic and Latino populations that would call South Bend home. It's a curious thing, but the densest Spanish-speaking population in St. Joseph County lives in a place named after Polish heroes, filled with Polish history, and drowning in Polish churches. All five of the historically Polish church buildings are still standing. They're all still used. They're just finding a different identity.

At the end of the ride, we're back where we started, a historic park in an old neighborhood that's becoming a new place. Casimir Pulaski was a hero, a Polish fighter in an American war. The park that bears his name was in the center of the part of St. Joseph County that became set apart for Polish American immigrants trying to make their way in the new world. It would be poetic to end our ride at some antique Polish restaurant, plates full of noodles, sausage, and potatoes. Only problem is that those places aren't here anymore and they haven't been for some time.

But I'm cold and I'm hungry and I've got to eat something. Fortunately for me, even though South Bend's past is ended, its present is here right now. Its present smells like tacos and tacos sound delicious. Just because a thing isn't the way it used to be doesn't mean that it can't be beautiful.

My friend Thelma is from these historic Polish neighborhoods and the tacos she serves up at Cinco 5 are the best ones in town. I can't feel my nose, but I'm ready to set my mouth on fire.

CHAPTER ELEVEN
THE VANISHING PARTS

After ten rides spanning more than 400 miles, it feels like I've explored all of the parts of St. Joseph County, but I know that I haven't. In fact, there's a whole corner of the map I haven't been through yet, and there's some pressure to visit it quickly. That's because, of all of the parts of St. Joseph County, it's the southeastern quadrant that's the most likely to disappear.

We're parked at that old landfill, the place now known as the Beverly D. Crone Restoration Area, and as before, I do not see any eagles. We jostle over the gravel of the parking lot, and in no time, we're rolling east on Johnson Street to explore the southern part of the county, but first we pause at the overpass to remember a quick bit of forgotten history.

Given the location of the portage, there was always going to be a settlement at South Bend. Mishawaka had iron and someday someone would have built a town there to mine it. Sumption Prairie had idyllic farmland and so did Granger. Even Osceola feels like an inevitability, given the resource of the river and Baugo Creek. There were always going to be histories at those places. But they very nearly weren't a part of the history of Indiana.

A historical marker at the intersection of Johnson Street and US 31 records the original boundary line of the Indiana Territory. In the earliest part of the 1800s, everything north of us – which includes South Bend, Mishawaka, and more than three-quarters of St. Joseph County's population – was considered part of the Michigan Territory.

When Indiana petitioned for statehood in 1816, they pushed to expand their borders. By drawing the new line just ten miles further north, the state would gain enough frontage to build ports on Lake Michigan as well as include both ends of the Kankakee portage within their lines. Michigan was not yet a state, and as such, had no representation in the Congress that would argue the decision.

Instead, the Wolverines had a stubborn streak and an apparent willingness to go to war. Michigan claimed for its own the northern ten miles of Indiana and the northwest slice of Ohio, including the city of Toledo. Militias were assembled from the three states, Hoosiers and Buckeyes willing to work together to defend the narrow strip of their turf from the encroaching Michiganders. Conflict was prepared for and expected. It might have been inevitable but for a compromise that was offered by the Congress. In exchange for relinquishing a narrow slice of its southern borders, Michigan would be given a large swath of land north and west of Mackinaw City, a place now known as Michigan's Upper Peninsula.

So peace won the day and Indiana's boundaries were redefined to include what would become South Bend, Granger, Mishawaka, Osceola, Notre Dame, Lydick, and New Carlisle. It may have been the most fortuitous political move in the history of St. Joseph County.

Across the overpass, we're into a place called Gulivoire Park. Once the target of one of South Bend's many failed annexation attempts, Gulivoire Park is surrounded on all sides by the city limits, but exists outside of them. It's little more than a collection of neighborhoods and subdivisions, a pair of churches, and a pair of schools. Nearly 3,000 people live here, with immediate access to the resources of the city but none of the taxes associated with it. On our bikes, it takes less than 90 seconds to roll through the full length of Gulivoire Park, and then, just like that, we're back into South Bend again.

We won't stay there for long. We cut through another neighborhood and sprint down York Street. The long fingers of the city don't reach past Kern Road, and by the time we turn onto Ironwood, the trappings of urban life are disappeared. We end up, like we always do, out in the cornfields. Only this time, it's the first part of an Indiana winter, the fields are barren, and the chilly crosswinds are whipping across them. There's nothing left to stop them from hitting us.

Down the road we run into a place called Woodland. It's not a town and I'm not sure what it is when I find it. The place is not much more than a slightly busier version of a rural intersection. Woodland has a crafty home goods store, two churches, and fewer than twenty homes. I know that last part because I counted all of them.

When Timothy Howard wrote his History of St. Joseph County in 1907, he was always optimistic about the small communities that became rural outposts between larger towns. When he wrote about Woodland, he said that Woodland had "always been a business center of some importance." He references schools and blacksmiths, grocery stores and a Post Office; even a doctor's office and four or five sawmills. I'm not calling Timothy Howard a liar, but there is not a hint of any of that as we cross the intersection that fully constitutes the unincorporated area of Woodland, Indiana.

In a matter of seconds, we're back into a grid of farmland and Woodland is over; but in truth Woodland has been over ever since the Wabash Railroad company plotted its route through St. Joseph County. Once they chose to pass through Wyatt, just two-and-a-half miles south of Woodland, the small town's fate was sealed.

Now, it's not like Wyatt is some urban metropolis either, but this is the country and there are levels to this. When the tracks were laid through Wyatt, it became a local hub for shipping and transportation. The two-and-half miles that separate the two communities don't seem like much, but for a farmer hauling a new plow that just arrived on the back of a train car, it would have been a big deal. In fact, it was a big enough deal to build one community and decimate another.

Wyatt is very obviously a rural community, and it makes no attempt to sell itself as anything different. But the long-term impact of even a long-defunct railroad is felt here, especially when you ride down from Woodland. Wyatt features a number of businesses, primarily in agricultural services. There's a fire department and a post office. There's even a gridded neighborhood, and not too long ago, there was a restaurant here, one that was allegedly housed in a century-old, haunted tavern. The restaurant may have survived the ghosts, but it didn't survive the pandemic.

Wyatt's importance was built on its identity as a stop on a rail line. Trouble is, it wasn't too long before the trains didn't stop here anymore. Now they don't even cross through Wyatt, and the line has been abandoned at least since the 1980s. When the last of the tracks were pulled twenty years ago, places like Wyatt became the only relics of the railroad era. It's a cautionary tale, and one that scares the hell out of the people who live in Lakeville.

You'll be unsurprised to learn that our route leaves Wyatt and into another agricultural zone, a redundancy of empty fields and cold winds. But things start to change once we're across US-31. Farms give way to neighborhoods and subdivisions. A handful of small lakes are visible through the naked trees, and a few minutes later we arrive in Lakeville, Indiana.

Lakeville might have developed like Woodland if the trains hadn't come through. Or it might have developed like Wyatt if the highway wasn't there. As it was, Lakeville had both. It was home to a depot on the rail line and the historic Dixie Highway was routed directly through its town center.

As cars came to dominate the American landscape and trains fell out of fashion, it was no bother for the people of Lakeville. Every person from South Bend and much of Michigan would need to drive through Lakeville to get to the southern part of the state or even the southern part of the country. Some number of those people would always need to stop for gas or a bite to eat.

Indiana's identity as the Crossroads of America was at its truest right here in Lakeville. Even when the railroad ceased operations, even when industry contracted and farms got bought by multinational conglomerates, Lakeville had a place on one of the most important thoroughfares in the northern half of the state.

Then they moved the road. The state of Indiana had promised for years to create a freeway between South Bend and Indianapolis, and when they finished the job, it trimmed as many as forty minutes off of the drive. I made the drive often, and it was a Godsend for me. But for the people of Lakeville, it threatened their very existence. There used to be 33,000 cars that passed through Lakeville every single day.

Not anymore.

We turn right onto the Dixie Highway, something that would have been unconscionable a decade ago. This road would have been filled with vehicles across all four lanes. It would have been death to cycle it. But today, like every day lately, the road is quiet. The shoulder is left uncleaned. People don't pass through Lakeville on their way to somewhere else anymore. You only get here if you're coming on purpose.

Their 2011 plan centered on the idea of transforming Lakeville into a bedroom community for South Bend, a scary proposition for those who appreciate the charms of their rural enclave, and a scarier proposition for those who wish the town could chart its own course.

Lakeville's history is tied up in reliance on something else, first the railroad, then the highway. To make itself into St. Joseph County's next suburb, they need South Bend to continue to create new jobs, something that's been far from a guarantee since Studebaker shut down in the 1960s. Even then, while Lakeville has made strides in establishing a set of beautiful parks, they're still missing many of the trappings of an attractive suburb, places like grocery stores, pharmacies, and chain coffee shops.

Even given all of that, the people of Lakeville, at least the ones I talked to, all seem hopeful for the future of their town. Over pints at the Lakeville Brew Crew, a microbrewery and neighborhood bar, I hear people express their thankfulness that the highway is gone. More incredibly, I hear the same sentiment from a man whose own house was razed to make clear the path for the new road, a mile east of downtown Lakeville.

Today the center of Lakeville is the kind of quaint downtown that carries the same charm and feel of plenty of small towns across the Midwest. It's filled with restaurants, cute shops, and a library. But until recently, it was a quaint downtown that was also filled with 33,000 cars, and at that point your town stops being so quaint. Its Main Street was impossible to cross. The idea of a neighborhood bar and a gathering spot on the Dixie Highway was something that couldn't have been imagined before the freeway was completed. But here we are, a dozen of us sipping porters, conversing freely about the beginning of deer hunting season, the virtues of conservative politics, and the greatest action films of the 1990s. I am well-versed in exactly one of these topics.

As my stay at the brewpub winds to a close, an older couple walks in the front door carrying a Crock-Pot and an Aldi bag. They unload their gear next to me on the bar top and then they leave. It takes a minute for me to process what just happened, and another moment for it to sink in. Like a late arrival to a church potluck, the couple had decided to drop off tortilla chips and homemade queso for the bar. We pass around bowls and scoop spoonfuls of dip. Turns out there's time for another pint. If this is small town charm, then sign me up.

It's hard to say whether the benefits of Lakeville's charm can make up for the economic loss of the tens of thousands of cars that used to pass through. It's surrounded by warning signs at places like Wyatt and Woodland. La Paz, Lakeville's neighbor to the south, with whom they share a school system, is all but dead; a sentiment that nearly every person in the brewery agrees on.

Lakeville exists in a kind of limbo right now, working toward an uncertain future, bereft one identity and trying to establish a new one. In fact, for all of its history, and there is plenty of it, Lakeville is now most famous for a decades-old murder, a story that's been picked up internationally thanks to the brand-new trend of true crime podcasting.

The Lakeville murders formed a sad and salacious story, a quadruple homicide that went unsolved for more than 25 years. But in 2016, a jury found Jeff Pelley guilty of killing his father, stepmother, and two stepsisters at the church parsonage where they all lived. Moments after the murders, he drove to pick up his date for prom and spent a night and a day in teenage revelry, dancing with his friends and then driving to Six Flags the next day to ride roller coasters as if nothing happened.

It's a grisly tale that only became more scandalous after 2020 when it was discovered that the elder Pelley may have had a shady past in Florida, possibly tied to cocaine trafficking. Indeed, one of his associates from his time in Florida was murdered execution style, just a year before the Lakeville prom night murders. That other murder remains unsolved and Jeff Pelley has continued to maintain his own innocence in this one.

Jeff Pelley's stepsister Jessica wrote a book in 2019, where she indicates that she believes Jeff is guilty of the crimes. His biological sister, Jacques, runs a website maintaining her brother's innocence. Jeff Pelley is scheduled for an appeal hearing in March of 2022.

None of this is anything you want to bring up with the people of Lakeville. There's some resentment that their close-knit, small-town community is associated with such a gruesome and bloody drama. Old-timers remember the incident as something they'd love to forget, except that the entire United States seems bent on conversating about it over and over again. For many, it's a nightmare that keeps happening. If the loss of the highway is the thing threatening to wipe them off of the map, you get the sense that they don't want the Prom Night Murders to be the thing that keeps them there.

Our ride out of Lakeville continues along the Dixie Highway, and I can't shake that something seems so wrong about cycling on this road. It feels like a swell of impatient traffic could line up behind us at any moment, but it never does.

We pass a home that claims to be the first log cabin erected in Lakeville, way back in 1836. The cabin's in there somewhere, I'm sure, but it's been remodeled and expanded and covered with vinyl siding along the way. Back into the farmlands, we turn left onto Osborne Road and toward a historic church. The Olive Branch

United Brethren Church existed on the boundary of the Huggart Settlement and was home to a community Sunday School that elected a black man – Andrew Huggart – as its superintendent more than 150 years ago. Unfortunately, that's not the history it's remembered for today. The parsonage next door is where four members of the Pelley family were murdered on a Saturday night in 1989, their bodies discovered the next morning by worshippers who were alarmed when the pastor hadn't shown up for church.

Lakeville is a town that's at war with its past, desperately trying to forget the parts that won't go away and sometimes trying to reclaim the parts that will never come back. Its roots run deep. The town was originally platted in 1857 by the son, nephew, and widow of Alexis Coquillard. Given that, maybe it's not surprising that they've cast their lot with South Bend.

In 1907, Timothy Howard wrote that Lakeville was a "place of rest and refreshment for the accommodation of travelers," and that's a lot of what Lakeville would continue to be for the next 100 years. And then, with the completion of a freeway, all of it was ripped away.

This corner of the county has been disappearing for a while. First it was Woodland, when the railroads skipped it. Then it was Wyatt, when the railroads left. The people of Lakeville don't want their town to be next, and I'm not sure how they'll do it, but good beer and homemade queso seems like a good start.

CHAPTER TWELVE
THE WHOLE THING

You never realize how big a place is until you try to ride all the way around it on a bicycle. And when it's just forty degrees outside? That only makes it feel that much bigger. The perimeter of St. Joseph County measures a shade over a hundred miles, and despite the lengths I've ridden during the first eleven rides, there are a few places I still haven't seen yet. We'll tick them off today, the second time we've tried to lick this ride.

The first time we attempted to ride the exterior of St. Joseph County, it was early August and temperatures were soaring into the mid-90s. Two of my friends ended up lying in ditches on the side of the road, dehydrated, cramping, and suffering from the intense heat. We ended up laid out in a yard somewhere near Bremen, hours behind schedule, and loading a friend into the back of an SUV as if he was a piece of luggage.

The second time was better.

Our ride begins from Granger and it ends in Granger, not for any other reason than that I live in Granger, and when this century ride ends, I want it to end as close to my own shower as possible. But I also realize something as I slip into my shoes and tighten the strap of my helmet. For as much as I've told the story of St. Joseph County, I've yet to tell the story of the place that's closest to home.

Maybe that's because Harris Township is a place with a relatively bland history; a set of farms that became a set of subdivisions, sprinkled with the expected conveniences of a modern suburb. Or maybe it's because there's more here than I want to confront, too many memories of days gone by, too many hurtful words ringing in my ear, all of it too much and too soon.

Whatever the reason, as we push off from the swanky shopping center at Heritage Square, my legs feel springy and I can't wait to get out of town. Of course, the problem with riding a circuit is that at the end, I have to come back.

We navigate suburban traffic through a pair of roundabouts, one of them wrecked down the middle by a car that must have treated the thing like a ramp. Soon enough we're off of the road and onto the Granger path. It's the place my kids learned to ride bikes and a week-and-a-half after I took my daughter's training wheels off, we did twenty miles along the path and the neighborhoods that connect to it.

A golf course cuts through a place that used to be a farm and one neighborhood after another sits proudly atop another place that also used to be a farm. In fact, with the exception of a handful of old farmhouses, the only other thing here that's appreciably old is the Harris Prairie Cemetery.

The prairie, the cemetery, and the township were all named after Jacob Harris, a man who has claim to be the first white settler in the place. You wouldn't know it by looking around today, but there was once an ecosystem here. The place even had elevation changes. Marshlands in the lower grounds fed nutrients into the farms on the high ground.

Harris would be appointed to the building of roads and would repurpose and rebuild a pair of Indian trails to connect his farmland to the world around him. State Road 23 was one of those Indian trails. Fir Road was another. It's a long ride today, but we still take a moment to peek at Jacob Harris's grave. And then, just like that, as soon as we cross to the other side of the cemetery, we're outside of the bounds of St. Joseph County. Or at least we would have been back in 1830.

The original bounds of the county ended at what is now Capital Road and, for a brief time, everything that is east of us right now belonged to Elkhart County, a strip of land that counted nearly 80 square miles. Elkhart County rejected the land. It was too wet, too swampy, too difficult to manage, and impossible to cross. So they ceded the land to St. Joseph County, and today, the eastern edge of St. Joseph County contains among the highest concentrations of wealth in the area.

Our bike path ends when we're spat out onto State Road 23 in the heart of the place called Downtown Granger. It's a misnomer, of course, a name applied facetiously. Technically speaking, Granger doesn't even really exist. It's not a town, it doesn't have a government, it doesn't have limits, and the people don't pay taxes to it. Maybe that's why it doesn't really have a downtown either.

By 1883, the railroads had come to Granger and a depot was constructed at the place that is now the Big C Lumber. Granger's early industrial aspirations were small and ill-fated. A factory was constructed near the depot in 1916, but the whole thing blew down in a windstorm. It would take another fifty years to clean up the mess.

For a time, this part of Granger would feature all of the trappings of a depot town. There was a hotel and a livery, a pool hall, even a pickle factory. But the railroads giveth and the railroads taketh away, and when the routes stopped coming and the trains stopped coming, downtown Granger began to evaporate. It would be fifty years before the suburbs would explode enough to bring it back again.

At Adams Road, we dash off of the congested shoulder of the highway and point ourselves due east. We can feel the farms bracing themselves against the onslaught of tidy subdivisions, each waiting to be absorbed by the residential phalanx that surrounds them on all sides. It's not that there's anything wrong with neighborhoods and I know that people need places to live, but it's in the nature of a subdivision to erase the history that lived beneath it. We turn right onto Ash Road, the County Line, where the encroachment of neat sets of manicured homes feels claustrophobic. I remember when this was the country, and as I'm buzzed by a shiny SUV, I find myself wishing it still was. Fortunately for us, it's a long ride and there are plenty of empty farms to come in the future.

A few miles up the road, we pass the oldest church in Harris Township as well as the newest school. The church near the corner of Ash and Brummit started out as the Salem United Brethren Evangelical Church in 1858, and yes, that's a very long name. That's part of why most of the locals called it "The Dutch Church", the other reason being its significant German population. In the 1890s, the church featured a Sunday School class taught in German. Curiously, the place used to have separate entrance doors for men and women.

Just south of the church is Discovery Middle School, considered the most elite school in a most elite school system. It's a prize to be able to send your kids there and if it doesn't produce the most popular bumper sticker among the cars that pass a little too close to me, it sure feels like it.

Just past the school we climb and descend the overpass that watches over the Indiana Toll Road. Built in 1956 and promised as the highway of the future, the toll road would separate neighborhoods in the city. Out here, it would divide farms right down the middle. Right now we're not far from the Maenhout Farm, the first piece of land to be sold in St. Joseph County to make way for the new road.

That's not to say that there wasn't excitement for the thing. Before it was even opened, cars lined up at toll booths for hours, and in some cases even days, to be among the first to have the privilege to drive it. I have to confess that I've never felt that same amount of excitement to do the same.

At Douglas Road, Harris Township gives way to Penn Township. The original settlers used to be afraid of this part of the county, remembering it as being so thickly wooded that it felt as if the sun never shone. The earliest settlers were prone to getting lost in making the journey from one cabin to another, but the people were tenacious. They'd manage to knock down enough of the woods to build the city of Mishawaka.

We cross the river and find ourselves back in Osceola, but only for a moment before we pass through its other side. I can't shake the feeling that Osceola feels like the part of the county that got forgotten, and maybe it wasn't just the broken dam of Alanson Hurd that made it that way. It's a place that was Michigan's before it was Indiana's and a place that was Elkhart's before it was St. Joseph's.

But before I can finish meditating on the unfair shake that the town of Osceola has been given, the town is over. We're fortunate to cross a busy set of tracks without incident or delay, and in a matter of moments, the sound of traffic is faded, and we are alone on the road. We're about to be absolutely entrenched in the middle of nowhere, and against all odds, after eleven bike rides spanning more than 500 miles, I am still ready to be surprised by what St. Joseph County has to offer.

The most remote part of St. Joseph County is almost certainly somewhere in Madison Township. It's the smallest township in the county, and it's barely half as large as the second smallest. It's miles away from any kind of town, something that's more of an inconvenience to a cyclist than a motorist. And of course, during our first attempt at this 102-mile ride, it's exactly where my friend Nate collapsed into the grass, convulsing in full body cramps that lasted for hours.

Madison Township was the last part of the county to receive settlement and judging by the looks of the place, it may not have happened even yet. Southern Madison Township is a time machine dotted with sheep farms and a country store. The road is covered in horse poop that's been flattened into the pavement by the tires of a dozen cars. At the corner of Beech and Shively, we run across an Amish schoolhouse, dotted with bike racks and actual hitching posts. The unincorporated bits of Nappanee poke through into the corners of Madison Township and St. Joseph County. The Yellow River, once a proud tributary of the Kankakee trickles through this part of the county. We cross it at a place that is now only called the Lateral Number Five Ditch.

For as much as Madison Township feels like a place separate from the rest of the county, it very much belongs. Like so many other places around here, a healthy portion of the township burned down during the 1870s, although in fairness, that probably only meant that about thirty people were affected. In fact, the place has been burning down all over again recently. Yard signs dot the lawns along the road, posted by insurance companies trying to suss out the culprits behind a string of barn arsons.

Although it doesn't count even a single convenience store or gas station within its confines, Madison Township does include a handful of agricultural businesses, communities at Woodland and Wyatt, as well as the largest landfill in St. Joseph County. If it wasn't for the Sunday morning church traffic, we might have ridden through the entirety of the place without seeing a car.

Beyond the dump, we cross over the freshly constructed US-31 bypass. Soon enough we're into a wooded area and we're skirting the lakes that gave Lakeville its name. After that, we're rolling south on the Dixie Highway and it feels like I'm 21-years-old making the long drive back to college after a holiday break. I still have days when I wonder if it was a mistake to come back.

The road is a ghost town, four empty lanes and a wide median to divide them. The shoulder of the road isn't cleaned anymore, and the wind is ripping the dust and detritus from the road and into my shins. We turn off the dirty highway and then there is nothing between Lakeville and Walkerton. Nothing at all.

Halfway into the ride, we pass through Walkerton. It's a place that's always seemed so far away from home, and with 50 miles to go, home seems far away from it. We pause to gaze upon the burnt shell of the Casey's General Station, where my nose bled and where people used to do their grocery shopping. Our route out of town passes a different set of similar looking farms, and as we skirt the edge of the county line, my GPS-enabled clocks bounce back-and-forth between time zones. It's an hour earlier at the houses on my left.

We roll past a sign beckoning us into the Place Trail Marsh. This was once a county park. Now it exists in a type of limbo within the Indiana DNR. It's another attempt to restore a section of the Grand Kankakee Marsh, although there is some concern that the animals are being shot as quickly as they can return.

By the early afternoon, even the Sunday traffic has dried up and now the sun is shining. We're turned north and the tailwind should push us the rest of the way home now. As we approach North Liberty, it's turned into a perfect ride on a perfect day.

And then the tires start exploding. Maybe it was debris from the cluttered shoulder of the Dixie Highway and maybe it was a rut in the road, but now we're flat at the North Liberty Library. There are worse places to suffer a misfortune.

With a fresh tube and a handful of fruit snacks, we're back on the road, along the continuous nowhere parts of the edges of the county. These are new roads and new places, and as I peer down each of the roads we're not traveling, I realize that there are still so many more places I haven't been. By the time this ride ends, I'll have traveled just 20% of the available road in St. Joseph County. It would take years to explore the rest of it.

St. Joseph County is not an excessively large place, but even during the course of this one ride, I feel each of the different ecosystems that we've traveled through today. The Kankakee Marsh has been vanished for more than 100 years, but its nutrients are still left in the soil. The trees shine more brightly with color, as if they've been Photoshopped into existence. The leaves hang on just a little longer. Between North Liberty and Crumstown, it feels if we've stumbled into a very short-term time machine. Here, thanks to the persistent gift of the expired marsh, the autumn is yet two weeks delayed.

But now we're hungry and we're in a bad place to be hungry. Madison Township may be the most remote township in the county, but the space between Crumstown and New Carlisle isn't far behind. Out here we find a car door, a television, and a whole collection of mini fridges tossed into a ditch. The roads are a crapshoot, some paved and some gravel. Somehow, a few of the gravel roads are better than a few of the paved ones. None of these roads feels wide enough for two cars. Maybe that's why that car door was in the ditch.

Somehow we wind up in a place where I do not know where I am. The roads have twisted and bent, changed names without warning. I'm not sure if our tailwind has become a headwind or if I'm going the opposite of the direction I expected. It's not that I don't trust my GPS unit. I'm just not sure I trust the guy that put the map in there. That guy is, of course, me.

It's a dangerous feeling when you've been taught to distrust yourself, trained to believe that in all circumstances and in all difficulties, it must be you who is at fault. It's a feeling and an instinct I've had to learn to ignore. I made this map, and if know how to do anything, I know how to make a map. We are not lost, I am not wrong, and you can't hurt me anymore.

It's a belief that I want to hold, but it's a belief that still requires proof, and I find that proof when the gates of Bendix Woods appear, exactly where they were supposed to be because that's exactly where I intended to take us. From there, I intend to go to New Carlisle, and that's what we do.

It turns out that I am not useless.

We roll into the town, intended once as a miniature Philadelphia, founded by an illiterate entrepreneur who would become a circus sensation on three continents. North of New Carlisle, we meet up with the Chicago Trail. Once a carriage path to a major city; now it's not really the fastest way to get anywhere. But we're cyclists and cyclists love this road. It's quiet, it's country, the asphalt doesn't suck, and most importantly, you can cruise this route for more than a dozen miles without a stop sign. Armed with a tailwind and a readiness for a hot shower, that's what we're going to do now.

For generations of Germans, the farms of northwestern St. Joseph County represented important slices of the American dream. You see whispers of that heritage in New Carlisle at Moser's

Austrian Café. It's in the names of the buildings and farms and roads that dot the landscape. There's no mystery in the nomenclature of German Township.

The small German town of Arzberg is nestled in the mountains near the border of Czechia. For years, Arzberg bounced back and forth between regional powers, sold to the Prussians, conquered by the French, later reclaimed by the Bavarians. During a period of massive turmoil throughout Germany, Arzberg received much of the worst of it. In order to prevent the poor from having children, strict laws were passed to prevent marriages among those deemed too destitute to do so. It was a bad time to live in Arzberg, and during the middle part of the 1800s, more than ten percent of its population left for America.

The vast majority of these wound up in South Bend. The Muessels were from Arzberg and so were the recipes for the beers that they brewed. The Elbels came from Arzberg as well, and our route takes us past the golf course that's named in their honor.

But the Elbels weren't known for golf. For a long time, they were known as the first family of South Bend's burgeoning music scene. In his History of St. Joseph County, Timothy Howard wrote that the Elbels were to music what the Olivers and Studebakers were to industry. They would found bands and choirs and orchestras. The Elbel Music Store operated out of downtown South Bend until the 1970s.

Beyond the golf course, we stumble onto the Carriage House, a fancy restaurant in the shell of the old German Brethren Church, once founded by Christian Holler's father. This used to be the center of the rural German community on the northwest side of South Bend. The Elbels played here with their cornet band. But the community isn't here anymore and it's an area that's becoming increasingly less rural.

A few hundred yards from the Carriage House we cross an overpass, and then we're into a place that's becoming more industrial. Pepsi has a facility where the farms used to be. So does Amazon. FedEx too.

It's not long before we're onto Brick Road, a road that was named after a lawyer and was never constructed from bricks. We're rolling back toward my old neighborhood, following the contours of my old school bus routes. If my legs weren't shot after the past 95 miles, I'd go the extra 400 yards to swing past my old house. But my legs are shot and so I don't.

I've been fighting cramps for the last hour or so, but the good news is that there's not much left. There are just eight miles between the house I grew up in and the apartment I live in right now. Somehow it's taken me a whole lifetime to get there.

We cross the river into Clay Township, a place named after Henry Clay, a senator from Kentucky. Historians call Clay the greatest senator in U.S. history, and he's ranked by one survey as the 31st most influential American of all time. I'm not sure if too many people who live here actually know that. I didn't.

It's barely a jaunt up the road before we pass the place where the North Village Mall used to be, a happy memory of the times when I would spend my meager paychecks on comic books. Now it's an assisted living center. Further up the road, there's the library that used to have the treehouse, but it's not the same library. The treehouse isn't there anymore either.

Nicholas Prathaftakis had a son would go on to be a founding member of the St. Andrew Greek Orthodox Church on Ironwood Road. We pass that church and then I think we pass the house that my first girlfriend lived in. Then there's the pool I used to swim at, the commute I used to make, and a hundred other pieces of history that are only a part of my story and not so interesting to anyone else.

Then again, they're not really a part of my story anymore either.

There's another church at the corner of Brick and Gumwood, once the site of the first airport in St. Joseph County. It goes without saying that the airport's not there anymore either.

And then the ride is over.

I stumble into the shower, collapse into the tub and let the hot water wash over me. My thoughts are not with the Studebakers or the Olivers or the Beigers. I am not concerned so much with Alexis Coquillard or Alanson Hurd or whichever decision makers decided to murder the Grand Kankakee Marsh. I've discovered a lot of history during these months and during these rides, but somewhere along the way, I realized I needed to confront another history:

My own.

So much of my own life has happened entirely within the narrow confines of this place, the fifth most populous county in the fourth most populous Midwest state. I was born here and I grew up here. I got married here and divorced here. It's where my life began and where I felt like ending it. God knows I thought about it.

I think I've decided that St. Joseph County is where it's time to start over again. There was a pretty girl on that bike ride today. In fact, she kicked my ass for most of it. I think it's time I ask her on a date.

ACKNOWLEDGEMENTS

I could have never written this book without the unwavering support of my friends, family, and coworkers. They pulled me out of a deep, deep funk and gave me permission to live again. To mom and dad, Sarah and Tim, Colton and Addy, Brian, Jacob, Lucas, Debi, Jared, and Paul; thanks. This book is for you.

To Andrew and Nate; thanks for being a part of my insane adventures and never balking at my craziest ideas.

Brian Sullivan, you saved my life.

Ashley, thanks for pushing me on my bike and pushing me to keep writing. You believed in all of this even when I didn't. Most of all, thanks for saying yes.

ABOUT THE AUTHOR

Aaron Helman is a cyclist, adventurer, and writer based out of Granger, Indiana. He is the author of <u>Simon Rousseau and the House on the Hill</u> and <u>First, Get a Million Dollars</u>.

Learn more about Aaron and his upcoming projects at aaronhelman.com.

Download the routes for each of these twelve rides at aaronhelman.com/stjoe.

Reach out anytime to aaron.helman@gmail.com.

www.ingramcontent.com/pod-product-compliance
Lightning Source LLC
Chambersburg PA
CBHW071313110426
42743CB00042B/1508